CONCILIUM

Religion in the Eighties

D1710306

CONCILIUM

Editorial Directors

Concilium 193 (5/1987): Religious Sociology

CONCILIUM

List of Members

Advisory Committee: Religious Sociology

THE CHURCH
AND CHRISTIAN
DEMOCRACY

Edited by
Gregory Baum
and
John Coleman

English Language Editor
Marcus Lefébure

T. & T. CLARK LTD
Edinburgh

October 1987
T. & T. Clark Ltd, 59 George Street, Edinburgh EH2 2LQ
ISBN: 0 567 30073 X

ISSN: 0010-5236

Typeset by C. R. Barber & Partners (Highlands) Ltd, Fort William
Printed by Page Brothers (Norwich) Ltd

Concilium: Published February, April, June, August, October, December.
Subscriptions 1987: UK: £24.95 (including postage and packing); USA: US$45.00
(including air mail postage and packing); Canada: Canadian$55.00 (including air mail
postage and packing); other countries: £24.95 (including postage and packing).

CONTENTS

Part IV
Development and Conflict

CONCILIUM 193 Special Column

Gregory Baum

John Paul's Visit to the Synagogue

Pope John Paul's visit to the Roman synagogue in April of 1986 was an important event in the life of the Church. The visit confirmed the new, ecumenical approach to Jewish religion adopted by the Church at Vatican Council II. In the celebrated paragraphs of Nostra Aetate the Council declared that God's promises remain with the people of the ancient covenant.

It was of course the Apostle Paul who in Romans 9–11 insisted that the covenanted Jewish community retained the glory, the covenant, the legislation, the worship and the promises, and that this people remained most dear to God on account of their ancestors, because God does not repent of his gifts. In the past, these Pauline passages were not understood as affirming that God's self-communication took place in the worship of the synagogue nor that God's redemptive grace continued to be offered in Jewish religion. On the contrary, Christians interpreted the Apostle Paul as saying that Jewish religion was now, after the coming of Jesus, an empty shell. The divine election remained with the people of God's first love, but this election was not a source of grace to them in the present. The election simply prevented them from falling into 'the world'; it kept them alive as an historical community; and it guaranteed that in the future, at the end of history, they would be saved in the unity of Christ's Church.

Vatican II offers a different reading of the Pauline passages. The abiding election of the Jewish people is now seen as a source of grace for the believing community. Nostra Aetate *speaks of a spiritual patrimony shared by Jews and Christians. It recommends mutual understanding, fraternal dialogue, and cooperation between Jews and Christians. Yet we note that it does not mention common prayer. At his visit of the Roman synagogue, John Paul II not only confirmed the new, ecumenical teaching, he went one step further. Following the logic of the new teaching, he prayed with the Jewish community.*

During the conciliar debate that preceded the adoption of Nostra Aetate, *many bishops opposed the new ecumenical approach to Jewish religion. In their submissions to the conciliar secretariat, they argued that until now the Church had always held that the Jews, refusing to believe in Jesus, were blinded, estranged from the source of grace and caught in a life under the shadow of death. Grace became available to Jews only if in fidelity to their ancient tradition, they accepted Jesus as the promised messiah. Some of these bishops complained that the proposed conciliar document tried to change the Church's perennial teaching. The simple faithful in their dioceses would be scandalised since they had always believed that salvation became available to Jews only as they turned to Christ.*

These bishops were right. The universally accepted teaching in the Church was indeed that the Jews had excluded themselves from the source of salvation by their refusal to believe in Jesus. This is how the New Testament message was read. This is what the Fathers of the Church taught in their sermons and writings. This was the common belief expressed in the liturgy and popular religious art. This was universally held in the Church. No Catholic teacher, until quite recently, ever proposed the idea that Jews have a living, spiritual patrimony which they hold in common with the Christian Church and which offers them access in faith to God's gracious self-communication.

Still, under the impact of what Vatican II called 'the signs of the times,' including the Jewish Holocaust, the Church has rethought its position. What light does the Gospel shed on the religious pluralism of the world? After Auschwitz, what light does this Gospel shed on the language of exclusion and the negation of Jewish existence that have characterised the Church's teaching over the centuries? Nostra Aetate *offers a reply to these questions. Interpreting the Scriptures in this new light, Vatican II concludes that God's grace is at work in the world religions and, in particular, that God's truth and grace are present in the spiritual patrimony of Jewish religion. Vatican II laid the doctrinal foundation for John Paul II's visit to the Jewish synagogue and his prayer in union with the Jewish community. How this recognition of God's grace in Jewish religion affects the Church's understanding of Christology is a topic still demanding attention.*

If we hold that the Church's fidelity to divine revelation implies the immutability of its doctrines, we should have to conclude that Vatican II and John Paul II have betrayed the ancient truth. There were in fact groups of Catholic traditionalists who protested against the pope's visit to the Jewish house of worship. If, on the other hand, the Church's fidelity to divine revelation is a dynamic, Spirit-guided process through which the Church draws upon this revelation to respond to the signs of the times, then the reinterpretation of ancient texts is possible, then the Church can change its doctrinal stance, then the Church can come to look upon Judaism as a sister religion, then Pope John Paul II can visit the Roman synagogue and pray with its congregation.

The Church's new, ecumenical approach to Jewish religion demands that Catholic teachers abandon the myth that the Catholic Church never changes its teaching. The perennial teaching on the Jews is a case in point. It has changed radically. We note, however, that the Church modified its teaching, not by compromising with the spirit of the world, but by appropriating the depth and richness of God's revelation discovered in a new historical situation. What the Church is discovering in these times is that whenever elements of the Christian religion are used to legitimate oppression, whether this be of Jews, of members of other religions, of women, or of lower sectors of society, then the liberating power of the Gospel, revealed in the death and resurrection of Jesus, demands the reinterpretation of these elements and the change of the inherited teaching.

Pope John Paul II's visit to the synagogue has far-reaching consequences not only for Jewish-Christian relations but for the wider struggle of the Church to free itself from all ideologies of domination.

Note that this Special Column, like others in this series, is written under the sole responsibility of the author.

THE CHURCH AND CHRISTIAN DEMOCRACY

Editorial

THE RELATION of the Church to political parties, while a topic of practical importance, is not treated in the Church's social teaching nor in ecclesiological treatises. It is the topic of this issue of *Concilium*. There are good pastoral reasons for this choice. For one, recent statements coming from Rome have forbidden priests to become identified with political parties and exercise leadership in them. Bishops and priests should stand for human rights and social justice and promote these Christian values among their people, but they must not appear to be 'partisan', i.e. identified with a particular political organisation. The Roman norm was applied very strictly in the Americas. Well known is the effort of the hierarchy in Nicaragua to remove the priests who were serving as ministers in the revolutionary government. Less well known are cases in the United States and Canada where Rome demanded that priests elected to serve as representatives in the respective legislative assemblies resign from their posts.

Many observers were puzzled by these Roman measures. After all, in the past the Catholic hierarchy had often been openly 'partisan', i.e. supported particular political parties. Pope John Paul II himself, who had stayed away from politics in Italy, decided in May of 1986 to give public support to the Christian Democratic Party.

Secondly, in Europe the existence of political parties that call themselves 'Christian' creates anxieties and problems of conscience for Christians who for Christian-theological reasons have opted for a different political orientation and support one or other political party of the left. These Christians often seek a certain distance from the Church. They resent the fact that the Church which has mediated the Gospel to them and to which they belong should be politically identified with a political party that, in their opinion, does not embody the Gospel ideals of social justice. This problem becomes particularly intense in countries where engaged Catholics together with other members of society promote a political project that is profoundly at odds with the social vision entertained by the political party blessed by the Church.

It would appear that the relation of Church and political parties is a topic that cannot be examined in an abstract, theoretical manner in reliance on an appropriate ecclesiology. The topic must be studied historically. As political parties emerged in the various nation States in Europe and on other continents, the churches reacted to them in various ways, depending in part on the degree of secularisation that pervaded political life. Subsequent developments of 'Church-party relations' in various countries cannot be understood apart from these earlier histories.

In this issue we focus on Christian Democracy. The historical debates about Christian Democracy deal with many of the political, theological and ecclesiological problems involved in the Church's relation to political life. We note that the term 'Christian Democracy' can be understood in two distinct but related ways. It could refer to the post-World War II political movement in Europe and Latin America and the corresponding political parties known as Christian Democracy. But the term could also be understood more widely as referring to all the political movements in the nineteenth and twentieth centuries that sought to bring together Christian faith and democratic practice, including the post-World War II Christian Democratic parties. The articles presented in this issue of *Concilium* deal with Christian Democracy both in the wider and the more specific sense. The articles by *Franz Horner*, *Walter Dirks*, *Daniele Menozzi* and *René Rémond* analyse the more recent political and ideological problems of Christian Democracy in the light of earlier historical developments beginning in the nineteenth century, while the articles by *Karl-Egon Lönne*, *Andrea Riccardi*, *Pablo Richard*, *Otto Maduro*, and *Michael Fleet* concentrate more directly on the post-World War II political parties and the debates and controversies associated with them, without however neglecting altogether the earlier histories.

The political controversies among Catholics include the debate regarding *Opus Dei*, an organised Catholic movement with an intense spirituality joined to a political vision and to political action. *Peter Hertel's* article offers an assessment of this movement of growing influence.

In his article on Christian Democracy in Europe, *Karl-Egon Lönne* offers an interesting explanation why in Anglo-American societies no political party has ever used the term 'Christian Democracy' to designate its ideal and its programme. He argues that since democratic practice was deeply rooted in Puritanism and subsequent Protestant formations, Christian democratic values entered into the cultural self-understanding of the English-speaking nations. All political parties, including British Socialism, lived within this consensus. And since this Protestant tradition demanded a certain separation of Church and State, yet opposed a totally secular society and a secularly-oriented government, the English-speaking countries never experienced the political secularisation and Kulturkampf that on the European continent produced the historical conditions in which the Christian political parties arose. This does not mean, of course, that in the Anglo-American world the churches do not exercise a certain political role nor that governments refuse to use religion for their own ideological purposes.

The articles by *Horner*, *Menozzi* and *Rémond* show that from the nineteenth century on, Christian political parties were creations of lay people who wanted to protect their Catholic identity and at the same time be open to the emerging democratic ideals. The Church tended to be afraid of these Christian Democratic movements. In most instances these movements, while firmly Catholic, were not interested in protecting the institutional privileges of the Church. They wanted the Church to be the source of the spiritual values that could become the foundation of a democratic society. Some of these movements even called for a more democratic practice in the ecclesiastical system itself. For these reasons, then, the Christian Democratic movements lived in some tension with the Church and occasionally were suppressed altogether. While Leo XIII's encyclical *Rerum novarum* of 1891 appeared to support Christian Democracy, his subsequent encyclical *Graves de communi* of 1901 limited Christian Democracy to charitable, non-political engagements to improve the social conditions. Several authors of this issue show that the official Church did not reconcile itself with democracy until the 1944 Christmas address of Pope Pius XII.

After World War II Christian Democracy emerged as a political force. Its principal aim was not the protection of Catholic identity in a secular culture but the creation of a more just and more value-oriented society. The founders of the movement had resisted Fascism before and during the war. Many of them regretted the Church's half-hearted response to the Fascist governments. In its affirmation of democracy and pluralism, Christian Democracy went further than the Church's official social teaching in those years. Yet Christian Democracy saw itself as the political expression of the reformist ideas of the pre-war Catholic Action movement, and in some countries the new political party was able to rely on Catholic Action's wide organisational network. Christian Democracy saw itself as a political project supported among its militant Catholic members by a particular spirituality.

At the beginning Christian Democracy endorsed policies of radical social reform. The political movement sought to build a bridge between the working class and the middle class,—the working class that had hitherto fought for social transformation in parties committed to secularism and the middle class that while open to humanistic and spiritual values had hitherto been unconcerned about the lot of the workers. In France this ideal was often formulated in personalist terms: Christian Democracy sought to overcome the individualism and the absence of social solidarity associated with Capitalism as well as the collectivism and lack of freedom associated with Socialism. Christian Democracy hoped that a strong government could constrain the Capitalist economy and make it serve the needs of the entire population, thus producing a qualitative transformation of society as a whole. Some of the original promoters saw Christian Democracy as 'a third way' between Capitalism and Socialism.

The bridging of differences between the constitutive groups proved to be extremely difficult. Christian Democratic parties tended to have two wings, one critical of Capitalism and reform oriented, and the other strongly anti-Socialist and identified with middle class interests. In Europe the vehement anti-Communist stance, promoted by conservative forces, including the Church, and supported by American financial aid policies, allowed Christian Democracy to become powerful very quickly in Italy and Germany, which meant that the parties became increasingly defenders of the *status quo*. It became possible to present Christian Democracy as the perfect anti-Socialist political strategy: it advocated social reform, opposed the class struggle, and aimed at reconciling workers and owners first in the same political party and eventually in the entire country.

Christian Democracy existed and still exists in many countries. It also has an international political presence. Since the number of articles in an issue of this review is limited, the editors had to make a choice. The articles on Christian Democracy in Europe by *Lönne*, *Menozzi* and *Rémond* concentrate on Italy, Germany and France.

Italy, as *Andrea Riccardi* writes, has been the great laboratory for trying out and testing the various ways in which the Church relates itself to political parties. While the debates taking place at the Vatican usually remain hidden from the public, Riccardi's article analyses a famous debate after the War, to which the public had access, between important church leaders, including Pope Pius XII and Cardinals Ottaviani, Tardini and Montini, on the role of the Church in relation to a Christian political party. Should Rome allow perfect freedom to the emerging Christian Democracy run as it was by lay people? Would such independence be harmful to the Church? Or should Rome seek greater control over the direction in which the party was moving? Should Rome favour the political unity of Catholics and thus enhance its own influence on Italian society? Or should Rome be content with political pluralism among Catholics, that is to say allow Catholics to choose the political party that corresponds best to their vision of social justice? The articles dealing with Italy show that under Popes John XXIII and Paul VI the official Church tended to leave greater freedom to the Catholic laity and distance itself from the Christian Democratic party, while at the present there is an effort on the part of the Vatican to exercise greater political control. Yet the articles also show that after the War the political impact of the Church on Italian society tended to wane. Catholics joined the parties of the left, Socialist and Communist, in great numbers and exercised a significant influence in them. More recently the referendum on divorce (1974) and that on abortion (1981) revealed how weak the Church's political impact has become.

In France, as we read in *René Rémond*'s article, Christian Democracy emerged after the War under historical conditions that were altogether unique and that explains why its political party, the Mouvement Républicain Populaire, eventually disappeared from the political scene.

Walter Dirks' article looks upon Christian Democracy in Germany from a critical perspective. The well-known German Catholic Socialist thinker and activist speaks for the outraged conscience of many German Catholics committed to a biblical vision of social justice and the radical stance taken by Latin American bishops and more recently even by the Church's official teaching: these Catholics must witness a party in their own country, that calls itself Christian yet is devoid of any reformist impulses. The German Church itself has forgotten that it is to be the salt and the leaven in society: instead the Church simply blesses the *status quo*.

The articles by *Pablo Richard*, *Otto Maduro* and *Michael Fleet* reveal Christian Democracy in Latin America was closely related to the European development but that the special historical conditions of the Latin American continent gave the Christian Democratic movement a distinct character. Special were the economic underdevelopment of the continent, the existence of masses of dispossessed people, and the remaining power of the old Church still identified with the land owners and the military. Christian Democracy began as a reform movement that stood against the feudal heritage, promoted modernisation, favoured a constrained Capitalism, and sought the support of the intellectuals, the new middle class and the urban workers (groups that had hitherto been secular and anti-clerical). As in Europe, Christian Democracy understood itself as a third way between Socialism and Capitalism. In Latin America, Social Democracy saw itself as a Christian political project, open to pluralism, that aimed at the transformation of the continent. Because the older, more traditional Catholicism was still strong, the modernising sector of the Church had to reorient the inherited Catholicism, develop a new Catholic ethos and spirituality,and articulate a Catholic social philosophy in support of the new political movement. Christian Democracy saw itself as a progressive force. While the secular, anti-clerical urban middle class and workers often accused Christian Democracy of aiming at the restoration of clerical power and traditional corporatism, representatives of the old Church often accused it of compromise with the world, with atheism and Socialism.

Christian Democracy in Latin America suffered from the same internal divisions as did the European parties. While the parties were in opposition, they promoted a progressive programme, but as soon as they came to power, 1964 in Chile and 1968 in Venezuela, they discovered that they were unable to guide Capitalist development and contain the power of the transnationals. And as they bowed to capital, they lost the support of their progressive wing. *Michael Fleet*'s article on politics in Chile shows that even as it resists the present dictatorship, the Christian Democratic party still wrestles with the same internal divisions.

What is new and unparalleled on other continents, we learn from the articles by *Richard* and *Maduro*, is the emergence of a Catholic, liberationist, political project, possibly still in a tentative phase, that defines itself against Christian Democracy. The liberationists argue that 'the utopia' of Christian Democracy, namely the creation of a just and fraternal society through the cooperation of the poor and the rich, is unrealistic and hence inevitably leads to frustration and failure. Liberation theology is therefore not simply a religious philosophy; it is closely associated with a new Catholic social project, religiously pluralistic in nature, that calls for taking sides in the social struggle, for the option for the poor, for preferential solidarity with the masses. What is remarkable is that recent Catholic social teaching—first the Latin American bishops conferences of Medellin and Puebla and later John Paul II's *Laborem exercens*—actually supports the preferential option for the poor and the more conflictual politics that flows from this principle. At the same time, after the success of the revolution in Nicaragua, the pressure on the liberation movements exercised by the defenders of the existing economic power, including the American government and at times a subservient Church, has become enormous. What the future will bring remains hidden in God.

Are there theological conclusions that emerge from these articles? It certainly appears that the Church has understood itself as a political actor in accordance with various models. At times the Church simply defended and blessed the existing order and intervened in public life only when religious and family values were disregarded. Yet when the order which the Church had defended over the generations was attacked by secular forces, the Church was sometimes willing to give public support to a conservative political party. In countries where Catholics were in a minority, the Church on the European continent was willing to support a Catholic political party to defend Catholic rights. The Church in the Anglo-American countries tended to see itself as non-political and exercise the role of a welfare organisation lobbying to protect the freedom and interests of its members.

Following a more theological inspiration, the Church in certain situations of crisis has seen itself as the promoter of a new social vision and new social values, accompanied by an appropriate spirituality. This was the situation in which Christian Democracy emerged. Yet from the beginning the official Church was uncertain whether to support the new vision and allow lay Catholics to define the direction of the new political party, or whether for the sake of the Church's own institutional interests, the hierarchy ought to exercise a restraining authority in the party.

The emergence of liberation theology confronts the Church with the same situation. The bishops conferences of Medellin and Puebla certainly saw the Church as a promoter of a new Catholic political project in Latin America. The bishops offered an ethical critique of liberal capitalism, projected a new social vision, favoured a less dependent, self-reliant economy, recognised the people as the historical agent of social change, called for solidarity with the poor, and made 'conscientisation' or the raising of consciousness part of the Church's pastoral ministry. Yet in this situation too the official Church was greatly divided. In Nicaragua, the bishops at first supported the struggle against Samoza and after the victory wrote a pastoral welcoming the arrival of Socialism, yet at a later time, worried about the Church's institutional authority, the bishops turned against the revolution.

It appears that the relation of the Church to the political order is entering upon a new historical phase. Recent Catholic social teaching not only fully endorses human rights and social justice and articulates a detailed ethical critique of capitalism but also presents its positions as grounded in and motivated by biblical revelation. This is new. The Church's concern for social justice no longer belongs simply to 'the natural order'. It is now seen as an integral part of its Christ-given, evangelical mission. It is this extraordinary doctrinal development that now pushes the Church in more and more countries to approach its political role in properly theological terms. Thus the Catholic Church in the USA and Canada—accompanied by the major Protestant churches—has become a critic of society and the promoter of solidarity and other evangelical social values. Yet after the bishops publish their pastoral pastorals, the debate among them continues. Should they give full support to their theologically-grounded social vision? Or should they give priority to the interests of the ecclesiastical institution, even if this means observing a relative silence on human rights and social justice? Today the Catholic Church is often afraid of its own social teaching.

The internal conflict in the institutional Church between biblical vision and institutional pragmatism explains the measures taken against priests who have assumed leadership roles in progressive political institutions. While they may well embody the Church's official social teaching, they are inconvenient to local bishops and Vatican churchmen who put the ecclesiastical organisation first.

A second conclusion derived from the articles collected in this issue is that Christian Democracy presents an excellent organisational model for the manner in which the Christian community (or any other religious community) could become an instrument of social reconstruction. Here is a political movement generated by Catholics, yet religiously pluralistic: it is alive out of a social vision of justice and solidarity, derived from Catholic values yet formulated in terms that have emerged in the political debate: it is supported by a spirituality and an ethos: and finally in building its power base, it can draw upon Christian networks and organisations and even count on the support of the official Church. Christian Democracy was guided by a Christian utopia, even if for historical reasons it has for the most part become a middle class party and the defender of the *status quo*. But the model itself remains attractive to the Catholic liberation movements in Latin America.

These movements see themselves as Catholic but ally themselves with secular and other religious groups; they work for justice out of a utopia inspired by the biblical promises but concretely formulated in terms of the contemporary political struggle; they possess a special spirituality and an appropriate life style; and they organise in clusters of base communities and in some instances have the support of the official Church.

The unanswered question that remains is how militant Christians inspired by the radical social teaching of recent Church documents can become agents of social change and bearers of peace in the capitalist countries of Europe and North America, fashioned to a large extent by the economic interests of the giant corporations, the exigencies of the nuclear weapons race, and the indifference of the middle classes to the present crisis.

Gregory Baum
John Coleman

Part I

Continental Perspectives

Karl-Egon Lönne

The Origins of Christian Democratic Parties in Germany, Italy and France after 1943–45

THE RE-ESTABLISHMENT of the Christian Democratic parties in the three countries focused on here is to be seen as influenced by the profound disruption caused by Fascism and National Socialism. Apart from the corrupting effect these ideologies had on secular politics and ethics, the wide variety of disruption they unleashed was brought about over two decades not only by the threat and the use of force but also by the temptation of a possible alliance with the formation of a common front against the political and ideological pluralism of the modern world or against some of its individual components like Liberalism and Communism, a temptation to which Catholics in these countries and the Roman Curia were exposed.

1. THE PRE-WAR YEARS

In Germany the coming to power of the Nazis in 1933 led in a few months to the forced dissolution of the Catholic political parties, the Zentrum and the Bayerischer Volkspartei.[1] The conclusion of the concordat between the Vatican and the Nazi Reich government set the seal, on the one hand, on the downfall of an independent political Catholicism but, on the other hand, could arouse the impression and the illusion that a *modus vivendi* had been found between the Catholic Church and the Nazi state so as to make possible for Catholics integration into the emerging Nazi State. But without any regard for the concordat the Nazis during the years of their domination unleashed a struggle against Catholicism and the Church which was waged with varying means and varying intensity and which led numerous Catholics to adopt a private attitude of opposition. Only in exceptional cases did this become politically active or even militant but in its intellectual and spiritual distancing from Nazism it represented an important factor of self-preservation which on the fall of the Nazi regime offered a fundamental pre-condition for a future contribution by Catholics to the re-shaping of politics.

In Italy in the mid-1920s the process took a little longer, but Fascism similarly used the same tactics of a combination of brute force and an opportunistic agreement with the Vatican to act against the Catholic party that had only recently been founded and had risen to political significance, the Partito Popolare Italiano or PPI.[2] The Lateran treaties of 1929 led, on the one hand, to the Church sanctioning the Fascists' political monopoly but, on the other hand, gave Catholics scope for religious activities and for running organisations connected with these, and in later years it was only in isolated episodic clashes that this freedom of manoeuvre was threatened and restricted. On the whole there was a rapprochement between Italian Catholics and the Fascist state to which the delimitation of spheres of influence laid down in principle by the Lateran treaties contributed to the extent that it did not only mean separation but also in many spheres suggested co-operation.[3]

The continued existence of strong Catholic organisations meant that leading Catholic circles also retained the possibility of taking a critical look at Italy's political and social development and of considering the future that lay beyond a possible collapse of Fascism. Centres of this kind of reflection were the Catholic students' and graduates' organisations, the Federazione Universitaria Cattolica Italiana and the Laureati Cattolici. In this context political analyses and objectives did not get a look-in. People concentrated rather on considering Church traditions and papal statements, with the help of which moral principles that had lapsed into oblivion would be brought to a new realisation in a Catholic State. A political expression of anti-Fascism was, on the other hand, represented by the illegal Neo-Guelf movement, which with its centre in Milan campaigned against co-operation between the Church and Fascism.[4] The leading anti-Fascist politicians of the PPI were paralysed by the ban on any kind of leadership within Catholic Action, but once Fascist pressure was discontinued they were able to perform an important task in reconstruction.

The party-political tradition of Catholicism in France was more recent and essentially weaker than in Germany and Italy. After the disputes surrounding the separation of Church and State at the turn of the century it was the national solidarity of the first world war that first led to the actual integration of Catholics in the Third Republic.[5] Catholics were strongly represented in the first post-war French parliament of 1919, even though they were divided among different political parties and groups. After lengthy preparations a parliamentary combination of thirteen Christian Democrat deputies was formed in 1924, and from this developed the founding of the Parti Démocrate Populaire or PDP. This party showed the influence of the PPI and its founder Don Luigi Sturzo. Thus it was non-confessional and was based on an anti-individualistic and organic image of State and society—a concept which through Sturzo had been given a fresh political realization. In the 1928 elections the PDP managed to reach a total of twenty deputies, but in those of 1932 and 1936 its strength fell back to half this number. The PDP advocated a moderate policy with a social emphasis and was among the opponents of the Communist popular front. It achieved only a modest significance and was not even able to attract to itself all Christian Democrats, let alone a substantial proportion of Catholic deputies. During the run-up to the second world war a new political grouping of Catholics obtained increasing importance, the Nouvelles Équipes Françaises, whose goal was to gather Catholics together and to renew democracy.

2. IN GERMANY

For various reasons it was particularly difficult to start things up again in Germany after 1945. Here the moral and material ravages that Nazism had left behind were particularly burdensome. It was not possible, as it was in Italy, for the opposition forces to prepare themselves over a longer period and relatively undisturbed for the collapse of the regime. After the end of the war the country was split into four occupation zones, which inevitably made a revival of political forces significantly more difficult. In the field of political Catholicism the impetus towards reorganisation came predominantly from former members of the Zentrum. Nevertheless there was just as little question as in Italy of an uncritical revival of the parties that had existed before the dictatorship. Rather earlier suggestions were taken up of making political Catholicism a component of a collective party that would bridge the confessions.

The most successful efforts at organisation occurred in Cologne.[6] The Cologne initiative was stimulated by discussions that had already taken place towards the end of the war in the neighbouring Walberberg priory between Dominicans and lay-people drawn from the former Zentrum. In subsequent negotiations the strong emphasis on a Christian Socialism as put forward by the Dominicans did not prevail. Nevertheless the Cologne principles maintained the demand for a 'true Christian Socialism'. Alongside the political demands for the rule of law and freedom of speech and opinion these principles also put forward far-reaching social objectives. They strove for a social incomes policy, a just distribution of wealth, and a certain amount of nationalisation in the interest of the general good. They went on to criticise large-scale industry and to call for the encouragement of small-scale ownership, particularly in agriculture.

Alongside the commitment to confessional co-operation there also arose an internal tension between, on the one hand, the circle of Catholics influenced by the Dominicans and interested in social reform, and, on the other, the Protestants, who predominantly joined the CDU from former political parties of the Weimar Republic that had stood further to the right. This was already noticeable in the influence of a Protestant circle from Wuppertal in connection with the formulation of the Cologne principles but also resulted in the success of Konrad Adenauer's efforts to restrain the social reformist tendency in the Christian Democratic Union (CDU) that was taking shape in favour of a controlled capitalist system, efforts in which he could count on the support of the party's Protestant circles.

The CDU's social reformist tendency nevertheless found strong expression once again in the Ahlen programme put out by the CDU in the British zone.[7] After detailed criticism of the industrial economy of the past, the programme formulated principles for the creation of an economic structure which in the interest of the development of the individual should be determined neither by an 'unlimited domination of private Capitalism' nor by its substitution by some kind of State Capitalism. In this way the programme opposed both capitalism and socialism and tried to find a third, middle way in their place. The over-great concentration of economic power was to be countered by limitations on corporations, cartels and share ownership. Nationalisation was demanded for coal mining and for the iron industry. The position of workers was to be strengthened by giving them a share in decisions and a right to information about the situation of the company. On social questions the works council should have a right to be heard. Planning and guiding the economy were accepted for emergencies but rejected as an end in itself. The entire new order was to be guided by the well-being of the people.

In the period that followed the idea of Christian solidarity developed by the Jesuits gained a certain importance for the influence of political Catholicism on the programme and activity of the CDU and of its Bavarian sister party, the Christian Social Union (CSU).[8] The concept of solidarity was originated by Heinrich Pesch and further developed by Gustav Gundlach and Oswald von Nell-Breuning, and it exerted some influence on the writing of the 1931 encyclical *Quadragesimo anno*. In it the common good and its demands were not placed so predominantly in the foreground as with the Dominicans'

Christian Socialism. Instead much space was given to the individual and to his or her development, even if his or her social links and duties were always taken seriously. It was flexible enough, on the one hand, to allow the development of Capitalist economic methods and, on the other, to emphasise the interests of the common good and the solidarity of society as a whole. State action at the various levels of society was accorded only a subsidiary and socially corrective function. Socialist and State Socialist tendencies towards regimentation were rejected as preparing the way for a disastrous collectivism.

The policies that prevailed in the American, British and French occupied zones of Germany and subsequently in the Federal Republic reveal that, just as in the internal development of the CDU/CSU, the originally strong momentum of social reform during the first years of its foundation were severely neutralised in its actual development. As in Italy and France, decisions were taken in favour of a neo-liberal system which owed its strong impetus to American economic and financial aid but which then developed a considerable dynamism of its own. It enabled the Federal Republic to achieve an unexpectedly rapid and large-scale rebuilding of its economy and laid the foundations of a considerable raising of economic and social levels which guaranteed for the most part the satisfaction of material needs but which for the most part left out of consideration structural criticism of the Capitalist industrial economy and its political and ideological implications.

3. IN ITALY

In Italy the distress of the situation brought about by the war and the expectation this gave rise to of the collapse of the Fascist regime led in 1942 to contacts being made by politicians of the former PPI both among themselves and with the Guelf movement, in which younger representatives of the Catholic students' and graduates' organisations and of Catholic Action were also involved.[9] A leading role in these activities was occupied by Alcide de Gasperi, who had survived the Fascist period as a Vatican official. He played a decisive role in the consideration of possible programmes by the discussion circles that were being formed, and in the context of these he worked out various programmatic statements.

The chief points were brought out in one of these papers of De Gasperi, which he called 'Ideas of Democrazia Cristiana (DC) for reconstruction'.[10] Political freedom was mentioned as the indispensable condition for the inviolable rights of the human person and for all civil freedom. It should be realised in the forms of representative democracy. Christianity was assured complete freedom of movement, since experience had shown that only its spirit of brotherhood could protect people from the catastrophes into which nations were led by totalitarian myths. The family and freedom of education were promised the protection of the State.

The greatest social effort should serve the goal of ensuring everyone not just food and work but also access to property. Unemployment should be brought to disappearing-point. Social security should be extended and its administration simplified. In industry the participation of workers in the profits, operation and capital of companies was demanded. Housing, education and opportunities for advancement would serve to de-proletarianise the working class. Given an industrial scene dominated by handicrafts and small and medium-sized businesses, these kinds of undertakings should be encouraged. The laws of ethics and of public interest demanded that the State should put a stop to industrial and financial concentration, 'the artificial creations of economic imperialism'.[10a] Further demands were the prevention of the concentration of the means of production and of wealth, and the suppression of monopolies or their being placed under public supervision or their removal from the private sector by being turned into co-operatives.

In agriculture several measures were suggested to encourage the formation of smallholdings owned by peasants or by co-operatives. A reform of taxation would help achieve a better distribution of property while taking into adequate consideration the interests of the middle classes. An entire section of the 'Ideas for reconstruction' was devoted to sketching out a system for representing people according to their professions or jobs, with a representative body alongside the political parliament. In what was said about foreign policy the themes were freedom and solidarity.

It has rightly been emphasised—a point that could be documented with additional material from De Gasperi's papers—that the stress on pluralistic political freedom established in the forms of parliamentary democracy went far beyond what the current tradition of Catholic social teaching was offering as a foundation at the time.[11] In the latter democracy remained one of the possible forms in which the proper goal of State activity, the benefit of the people, could be made possible. De Gasperi linked his demands for freedom and democracy historically to the French Revolution and by way of Italy's Catholic liberal tradition tied them in with the liberal movement. He thus anticipated a development which was only to gain more general significance within Catholicism in later years with a new appreciation of human rights. Even his economic ideas went beyond Catholic social teaching by raising concrete demands which took into account the criticism of Capitalism that had been intensified in the wake of the world economic crisis.

De Gasperi's ideas about a special vocational system, in other words a corporative system, show the extent to which such ideas had been reinforced in the thinking even of Italian Catholics by the encyclical *Quadragesimo anno*, even though the corporative practice of the Fascist State was designed to discredit any idea of organisation along vocational lines aimed at achieving political freedom and economic equality.

If one compares the programme De Gasperi was putting forward with how Italy actually developed during the post-war period, one cannot overlook the great contrast between them, even when one takes into account the probability that De Gasperi could count on realising the objectives set out in his programme only slowly and step by step. This contrast arose even though De Gasperi took over as head of the Italian government in 1945 and the DC as the strongest political force provided his eight cabinets up to 1953 with their chief foundation.

Various factors are to be adduced to explain this divergence between the programme and how it was realised in fact. First of all it should be remembered that the programme wanted to mobilise all the country's forces in the service of reform. But the end of the war brought with it a slump in the Italian economy which could only be overcome with large-scale aid from America and which was transformed into an originally modest prosperity by the liberal economic policies of Luigi Einaudi and others. In this situation attacks on monopolies in an economy that was now getting on its feet again seemed just as unsuitable as proceeding against the concentration of financial and economic power. It was not by chance that De Gasperi continually talked of the great importance of production.[12] In the implementation of policy an increase in production was needed to provide the basis on which depended the government's future ability to act.

Finally it has been convincingly demonstrated that within Italian Catholicism a movement in favour of the Capitalist development prevailed. This arose from aspects of Catholic spirituality that favoured mastering the tasks of shaping this world.[13] Traditionally and as a programme it drew on the basis of Catholic social teaching to formulate contents such as we have noticed in De Gasperi's programme but which were emphasised by politicians from the circle around Dossetti,[14] although they could only be seen as general perspectives for the future.

Agrarian reform belonged both to the tradition and to the programme of the DC. What militated against it, besides the paucity of the means that had to be mobilised, was the fact that the DC could not come out emphatically on the side of the rural lower classes since it had to present itself as a party that transcended class and social differences if it wanted to add to its traditional agrarian support the classes that had previously stood particularly closely among the followers of Fascism.

De Gasperi's political achievement consisted of having produced a broad democratic consensus in the precarious situation of the fall after so many years of the Fascist régime and defeat in the war. This consensus outstripped the alternatives both on the side of revolution and on the side of reaction. But this meant that the realisation of the original efforts at reform were only very limited and hesitant.

4. IN FRANCE

In France the Vichy regime that collaborated with the German occupation showed itself accommodating towards Catholicism.[15] But that did not stop numerous Catholics who had often been shaped by the Christian Democrat groups of the pre-war years joining the Resistance when it emerged. The efforts to establish the Mouvement Républicain Populaire (MRP) in 1944 stemmed from the Resistance. This party quickly developed into a third political force alongside the Conservative right and the Socialist or Communist left. It began by winning the support of up to a quarter of the electorate but lost ground steadily from as early as 1947 onwards. The party did not want to remain confined to Catholics. But in practice it was led by committed Catholics and gained its support mainly from among Catholics. With the MRP France for the first time, even if only for a limited period, had a large-scale party of Catholics: in other words a party like that which had developed in Germany, even if with much stronger links with the Church, as early as 1870 and in Italy for a brief period in the 1920s.

The MRP was inspired by the ideas of Catholic social teaching without going out of its way to stress its dependence on them, since it consciously wished to appeal outside Catholic circles. It tried to overcome the traditional opposition in France between conservative Catholicism and progressive Republicanism. It wanted to develop and disseminate an independent intellectual and political awareness and thus to contribute to the re-shaping of French society, economy, and politics. The MRP recognised the Revolution of 1789 and wanted to supplement and renew it by drawing on the traditions of a Catholic personalism. Thus individual freedom should be extended from politics to the economy and society and not be regarded as achieved by the isolation of the individual within the State and society. The individual's personal development should be encouraged by the State, recognising and protecting his or her involvement in such social groupings as the family, the parish, and the place of work. The person and society were thus seen as being in an organic relationship to each other. The development of the individual should not be impeded or even made impossible by the claims of the economy or the State. This meant that individuals should not be handed over to economic exploitation. Instead they should be helped to share in the shaping of modern industrial society by sharing in the running of the companies in which they worked, and they should be strengthened economically by a more equitable distribution of income with the aim of achieving greater social justice. The polarisation of society between rich and poor should thus be done away with and those who were economically disadvantaged should be liberated from their dependence. Men and women should be able to act as rational and responsible members of society in the economic world as well as in society as a whole.

The personal definition of men and women in their actual social relationships was meant, on the one hand, to overcome liberal individualism, which may have given the individual political freedom but for the rest handed him or her over to social isolation and the vagaries of economic success or failure. On the other hand, the personalist view of man was meant to overcome the collectivism of Socialism and Communism, which turned the individual into a component, insignificant in itself, of a collective society in which the authority of the State was turned into an absolute, even if in the hope of a free society to be reached at some indefinite time in the future. Catholics were thus to be brought not just to accept democracy but to develop it by their contribution in the sense of Christian democracy.

When it came to solving actual economic and social problems the MRP could not prevail against the other and stronger political forces but was obliged to enter into a variety of compromises which meant that its own goals remained unfulfilled. In this way the MRP was for many years a sought-after and often indeed indispensable partner in the building up of a parliamentary majority, but it remained and became increasingly the junior partner in governments which it was able to influence over individual problems but on which as a whole it was unable to set its stamp. In keeping with this development French Catholics as early as the 1950s, and increasingly in the 1960s and 1970s, reverted to the tradition of dividing their votes among a wide variety of political parties and hardly attempted any more to exert influence on political decisions as a substantial solid grouping. However this did not mean that their ethical and political contribution was ineffective and unimportant even in this situation.

The lessons to be drawn from this sketch of the political situation of Catholics in these three countries is that the crisis they found themselves in, partly buttressed by the tradition of Christian social teaching but also going beyond this in some important points, inspired them to promising proposals for reform which had been demanded by the domination of Fascism and Nazism and by their catastrophic effects. For the most part these proposals for reform were blocked as a package by the development which actually occurred of a neo-liberal economic policy with its social, economic and political requirements. However the picture would only become complete if one were able to trace in detail how individual proposals for reform did have effects despite being modified, delayed, and brought about by circuitous means, and thus contributed to the emergence in these three countries of patterns of social order which have a not insignificant series of positive entries to show for themselves and which should be capable of adding to them in keeping with the needs of the times.

Translated by Robert Nowell

Notes

For the whole subject cf. K. E. Lönne *Politischer Katholizismus im 19. und 20. Jahrhundert* (Frankfurt-am-Main 1986).

1. R. Morsey *Der Untergang des politischen Katholizismus. Die Zentrumspartei zwischen christlichem Selbstverständnis und nationaler Erhebung 1932/33* (Stuttgart/Zürich 1977).

2. G. de Rosa *Il Partito Popolare Italiano* (Rome 1969).

3. P. Scoppola *La proposta politica di De Gasperi* (Bologna ²1978).

4. C. Brezzi 'Movimento guelfo' in *Dizionario storico del movimento cattolico in Italia 1860–1980* ed. F. Traniello and G. Camparini, I, part 2 (Turin 1981) pp. 333–335.

5. J. M. Mayeur *Des Partis catholiques à la Démocratie chrétienne, XIXᵉ–XXᵉ siècles* (Paris 1980).

6. H. G. Wieck *Die Entstehung der CDU und die Wiedergründung des Zentrums im Jahre 1945* (Düsseldorf 1953).

7. *Dokumente zur parteipolitischen Entwicklung in Deutschland seit 1945* ed. O. K. Flechtheim, II (Berlin 1963) pp. 53–58.

8. R. Uertz *Christentum und Sozialismus in der frühen CDU. Grundlagen und Wirkungen der christlich-sozialen Ideen in der Union 1945–1949* (Stuttgart 1981).

9. P. Scoppola, the work cited in note 3.

10. *Scritti politici di Alcide de Gasperi* ed P. G. Zunino (Milan 1979) pp. 256–263 'Idee ricostruttive della Democrazia Cristiana'.

10a. *Ibid.* p. 259; 'creazioni artificiose dell'' imperialismo economico'.

11. P. Scoppola, the work cited in note 3.

12. P. Barucci *La linea economico-sociale: De Gasperi e l'età del centrismo (1947–1953)* (Rome 1984) pp. 143–161, 157–158.

13. A. Giovagnoli *Le premesse della ricostruzione. Tradizione e modernità nella classe dirigente cattolica del dopo-guerra* (Milan 1982).

14. P. Pombeni *Il gruppo dossettiano e la fondazione della Democrazia Cristiana Italiana (1938–1948)* (Bologna 1979).

15. F. Goguel 'Christian Democracy in France' in *Christian Democracy in Italy and France* (Notre Dame, Indiana, 1952) pp. 107–225; J. M. Mayeur, the work cited in note 5.

Pablo Richard

Political Organisation of Christians in Latin America: from Christian Democracy to a New Model

IN LATIN America, the majority of the population is both *poor* and *Christian*. This is why reflection on the *political efficacy* of faith and on the *political responsibility* of Christians is so important. In the past, in some countries and for some Christians, Christian Democracy offered a real possibility of political militancy. Later, this model entered on a period of crisis. Today in Latin America we see clearly that it is both inopportune and illegitimate to create a new Christian political party, but it is also inopportune and ineffective to leave the political militancy of Christians to individual decision or the free play of political forces. Christians today have become part of the political project of the poor, with all their organic and political richness, and this has taken the place of the project based on an idea of Christendom and Catholic political organisation. But this inclusion in the project of the poor and this militancy have to be carried out in a thought-out and collectively organised form by the churches if Christians are to go on being active and adult members of their Christian community while, at the same time, being able to bring a structured and public contribution, as Christians, to the political project of liberation of the poor.

   This article is divided into three parts. In the first we look at the political opportunity for Christian Democracy in the past. In the second we analyse the causes and effects of the later crisis of Christian Democracy. In the third, the longest and most important, we analyse the historical conditions and the elements that make up the new model of political organisation of Christians in

Latin America. This model, as we shall see, definitively replaces the concept of a Christian political party.

1. THE POLITICAL OPPORTUNITY FOR CHRISTIAN DEMOCRACY

Beginning in 1930, but most in evidence in the fifties and sixties, the whole of Latin America saw the rise of a new political project. In some countries Christian Democracy was to form a model of a political party that would allow many Christians to take an effective role in this new political project. This historic opportunity for Christian Democracy had positive results for Christianity in Latin America at that period.

This new political project was *reformist*, normally known as *populist*, and in its final phase also seen as *developmentist*. It was opposed to the earlier oligarchic regimes, conservative, élitist and authoritarian in nature, which had been dominant in Latin America generally between 1880 and 1930. The new project took shape in Latin America with the processes of industrialisation, democratisation, modernisation, urbanisation and all the new social and political reforms; its agents were the creole bourgeoisie, backed up by the growing middle classes, allied with some sectors of the popular classes. Populism thereby represented a broad social reformist pact in which the middle classes took the leading role.

The political opportunity for Christian Democracy in Latin America arose within this reformist-populist-developmentist political project. Not in all countries, but mainly in those where the new political project had reached a middle stage of development. Christian Democracy did not take root in the big countries such as Brazil, Mexico or Argentina; nor in most countries where the new political project took little root. Christian Democracy developed furthest in Chile and Venezuela. In Chile the National Falange was founded in 1938, changed into the Christian Democrat Party in 1958 and won power in 1964. In Venezuela the Christian Social Party was founded in 1946 and came to power in 1968. Christian Democrat parties, though with little political significance, were also founded in Peru and Guatemala in 1955; in El Salvador, Panama and Paraguay in 1960; in the Dominican Republic in 1961 and Uruguay in 1962, Costa Rica in 1963, Ecuador and Colombia in 1964, etc. Starting from its *European tradition* (with more than a century of experience: Lamennais, Lacordaire, Ozanam, Maret; and later Luigi Sturzo, Marc Sangnier, De Gasperi, etc.) and based on the social teaching of the Church (starting with the encyclical *Rerum Novarum* by Leo XIII in 1891) Christian Democracy in Latin America went on to form political parties coherent with the new populist-developmentist political projects of the thirties to the sixties.

The elements that ensured its coherence with this new political project, and therefore explain its political opportunity over this period, are the following:

(a) the multi-class nature of the new movement, arising from the new alliance between the bourgeoisie, the middle classes and some sectors of the popular classes, in contrast to the declining single-class oligarchy which preceded it;

(b) the reformist and developmentist ideology of Christian Democracy, which allowed it to escape from the traditional struggle and polarity between conservatives and liberals. Christian Democracy thus managed to go beyond traditional ideological conservatism centred on the family and schooling and to open itself to social questions;

(c) its populist stance, which allowed it to escape from the élitism typical of the earlier oligarchy and open itself to middle and working class sectors (without breaking with the ruling capitalist system);

(d) its new political institutions, which were an advance on those of the previous oligarchic State and marked progress towards a new State with a greater degree of democracy and participation.

This coherence between Christian Democracy (with its European tradition and basis in the social teaching of the Church) and the new political project, which produced its political opportunity, corresponded to very positive changes coming about in Latin American Christendom. By Christendom I mean the model of integration of the Catholic Church in society. In many countries the development of Christian Democracy corresponded to the change from a conservative Christendom to a reforming Neo-Christendom, which placed the Church in a very favourable situation. In conservative Christendom the Church was involved in civil society, concentrating on the family and school in its pastoral work; now, with the development of a reforming Neo-Christendom, the Church also acquired a presence in political society, following an aggressive pastoral approach in the social and political areas. Before, the Church had been the captive of oligarchic élitism; now, it was opening out to the middle levels without breaking with the dominant bourgeoisie. Before, the Church had expressed a defensive and conservative ideology struggling against liberalism and positivism for a century; now, the Church could take up an attacking, reforming ideology consistent with the social teaching of the Church but without breaking with the Capitalist system. Before, the Church had lived on the margins of the State, which was usually in the hands of a liberal anti-clerical oligarchy; now, the new democratic-populist State sought the support of the Church, took up its social teaching and assured all its civil and social rights. Never had the State-Church alliance functioned better than in these years. To sum up, we might say that between the thirties and sixties, in some countries of Latin America, there was a coherence between the new political model, the development of Christian Democracy and positive changes in the Church which together produced the rise of a new model of Christendom: reforming Neo-Christendom. Never before in its history had the Church felt itself to be in such a favourable and dynamic situation, and this is why it enthusiastically endorsed the Christian Democrat programme and, through Christian Democracy, the new political programme. The political opportunity of Christian Democracy in this period is explained by this coherence with the populist-developmentist political programme and by the support it received from the Church in Latin America. In some countries, such as Chile and Venezuela, this coherence and alliance between civil society, political society and ecclesiastical society, came to be expressed in a triumphalist manner. Here Neo-Christendom reached the heights of its development and was supposed to have produced a definitive model.

2. THE CRISIS OF CHRISTIAN DEMOCRACY

Towards the end of the sixties and throughout the seventies Christian Democracy came to the end of its period of political opportunity and found itself, instead, in a period of crisis and an accelerating process of partisan perversion. In Latin America we went all too quickly from opportunity to crisis and, finally, to perversion of the Christian Democrat project. Let us briefly look at the causes and effects of this historical process.

The causes of the crisis and the waning of the political opportunity of Christian Democracy are the following:

(a) The exhaustion of the reformist, populist, developmentist political programme within which the political programme of Christian Democracy had unfolded;

(b) the rise of a new model of *domination* opposed to the model of society put forward by Christian Democracy and the social teaching of the Church. This new model of domination excluded the majority of the people from economic life, transformed the democratic State into an authoritarian State of National Security and condemned the middle classes to disappear from the political life of their nations;

(c) the birth of a new model of the Church within the popular movement, generally called 'The Church of the Poor'.

So while Christian Democracy had developed at the outset of reformist Neo-Christendom, now with the crisis of this model of Christendom and the rise of a different model opposed to the Christendom model, Christian Democracy lost its place in the social and ecclesial context of Latin American history.

The effects of this crisis of Christian Democracy and the survival of a party which has lost its political opportuneness are the following.

(a) In political life Christian Democracy serves as an agent legitimising the new system of domination. It looks like an alternative to regimes of National Security, but in fact, going beyond appearances, it upholds and legitimises the present system of domination. The most obvious and tragic case of this is El Salvador, in which Christian Democracy has come to cloak and legitimise a military regime carrying out a terrible war of repression against the people of the country. The military provide the power and Christian Democracy its ideological cloaking. So Christian Democracy has come to be an implement legitimising the most terrible repression being experienced by the people of Central America. What is striking in this situation is the partisan and political perversion undergone by Christian Democracy in El Salvador, where it is seen to be an accomplice of violence and corruption. It is beginning to find itself in a similar situation in Guatemala. In Chile too, Christian Democracy may play a similar part if it accepts being an alternative to Pinochet, while upholding the same oppressive and repressive system. Here Christian Democracy runs the risk of prolonging the Pinochet-style system, without Pinochet.

(b) This Christian Democracy in crisis, with no genuine political opportunity and in a process of political perversion, is politically confusing to the hierarchical Church, making it believe that the era of Christian Democracy is still something current and possible. Besides confusing the Church and making it an accomplice of a great deal of violence against the people, Christian Democracy is deeply distorting the social teaching of the Church by trying to adapt it to be a legitimising authority behind the new model of domination.

(c) Christian Democracy, in this process of crisis and perversion, is coming into open confrontation with the political programme emerging from the popular movement; it is also in open contradiction with the massive presence of Christians within the popular movement and with all the spiritual, pastoral, theological and ecclesial richness which this Christian presence in the midst of the poor signifies. The politics of Christian Democracy is thereby contradicting the process of Church renewal as found in the second Vatican Council, in the Latin American episcopal conferences of Medellín and Puebla, and in the development of the base Christian communities and the theology of liberation.

In short, Christian Democracy is progressively contradicting the processes of liberating transformation found as much in society and politics as in theology and the Church.

3. THE NEW MODEL OF CHRISTIAN POLITICAL ORGANISATION

Christian Democracy is in crisis, it has outrun the historical time of its political opportunity and has started on a process of partisan perversion, which makes it the accomplice of the violence and corruption of the ruling political system.

All this is clear, but what is the alternative? It is not enough to say 'No' to Christian Democracy. We need to create a new model for Christians to organise themselves politically. There will always be a collective obligation on Christians to make their faith politically effective in a poor and Christian continent such as Latin America. In the past, in some countries, it was legitimate and effective to operate within Christian Democracy; it was even the choice made by many seeking a positive, indeed even revolutionary, political commitment. Today Christian Democracy no longer offers this possibility of operating in a way consistent with history, faith and the social teaching of the Church. What then is the alternative? The exhaustion and disappearance of Christian Democracy as a possibility for Christian endeavour has left a vacuum which needs to be filled. Christians cannot be encouraged to seek individual, spontaneous solutions or to proclaim the end of any public organised action by Christians who take part in politics in the name of their faith. In the following pages I will attempt to define a *possible new model* for political organisation by Christians, going beyond the Christian Democrat model and definitively taking its place.

First, we need to define the historical, political, theological and ecclesial conditions of this new model for political organisation by Christians in Latin America.

(a) The new model should take the political project for the liberation of the poor as its historical point of reference. The earlier reformist, populist and developmentist programme no longer exists, and the new model of domination is clearly contrary to Christian faith and the social teaching of the Church. The only reasonable alternative is the historical project of the poor, who make up the majority of people in our continent. This project is clearly not completely defined, but Christians should not wait for it to be defined to take part in it. We should take part from now in order to have the right to define it better and even to improve it from the standpoint of our Christian faith. Any model of Christian political organisation should lead us to become more entrenched in the programme for the liberation of the people.

(b) This new model must finally take the place of the Neo-Christendom model. In the latter, the Church still considered itself allied to political power and needing to hold more power; the world was still seen as part of the Church as the-world-of-the-Church, and this produced the need for Christian institutions: Catholic schools, Catholic universities, Catholic trade unions, Christian popular movements and also a political party belonging to the Church and serving the Church. This Neo-Christendom model has been completely superseded by the recent renewal of the Church and by the historical evolution of the popular movement itself. The Church can no longer go on using political power in order to assure its presence in society, but must rely solely on the strength of its faith, hope and charity; on the strength of the Gospel. The Church must seek to become part of the world of the poor, to be the leaven in the dough, with all the liberating power of the Gospel, by exercising this spiritual power which is proper to it.

(c) Besides being a part of the historical programme of the poor and definitively taking the place of the Neo-Christendom model, the new model for Christian political action must be consistent with the present movement of renewal in the Church, expressed as much in the official documents of the Church as in the life of the base Christian communities with all their spiritual, pastoral, theological and doctrinal richness.

It is not possible to give an overall outline of this new model of Christian political organisation in Latin America here, since it is emerging slowly in tune with the movement of history and the advance of its liberating processes. But the experience that has been built up over approximately the last fifteen years is very rich and varied, sufficient to give us a clear idea of the sort of model that is emerging. What follows stems from my own experience in Central America, which has its own particularities, although not so different from what is happening in the rest of Latin America. Rather than a theoretical definition of this new model I will give the *historical elements* out of which it is at present being constructed.

(a) The common political programme of liberation

The first element is the common political programme being carried out by Christians and non-Christians within the project of the liberation of the poor. Christians and non-Christians who adopt a liberating, even revolutionary, political stance find a mutual identification, discovery and respect. In this common experience, shared to the ultimate consequences, including death, Christians neither hide their faith nor use political practice as a means of religious proselytism. Ernesto Guevara said, in words that have become prophetic: 'Christians should opt definitively for the revolution, particularly on our continent where Christian faith is so important to the masses; but, in the revolutionary struggle, Christians cannot seek to impose their own dogmas nor to proselytise for their churches; they should come without any claim to evangelise Marxists and equally without the cowardice of hiding their faith so as to be like them. When Christians dare to give a complete revolutionary witness, the Latin American revolution will be invincible, since till now Christians have allowed their teaching to be used by the reactionaries.' Equally, Marxists have discovered Christians and the liberating political power of faith; they have renounced atheistic proselytism. Today in Central America we no longer talk of 'Christians and Marxists', but of *revolutionary Christians and non-Christians*', so as to avoid ideological contrasts and emphasise common practice in which each recognises his or her own identity.

(b) The presence of a relevant spirituality, pastoral practice and theology

The second historical element in this new political Christian organisation is the existence of a spirituality, pastoral practice and theology with which politically militant Christians in the popular movement can identify. Without such identification this new model would be impossible. Without it committed Christians either abandon their faith and their Church community or simply privatise their faith (reduce it to a private or family affair), thinking that faith has nothing to contribute to political action or that it is something superfluous hindering the political programme of the poor. In Latin America, and most especially in Central America, militant Christians normally belong to a base community in which they find a spirituality, pastoral life and theology which allow them to go on maturing their faith within the political practice of liberation. What is coming to life is a new way of looking at faith, the Church, the Bible, the sacraments, etc., consistent with political militancy. Not only is it consistent, but it also possesses the proper and necessary dynamism to fertilise and deeply transform political practice itself. Their faith makes militant Christians discover the utopic and transcendent dimension of political practice.

(c) The political diaconate of the Church of the Poor

The third historical element is what in Central America is usually called the political diaconate of the Church of the Poor. The Church provides a political service to the popular movement, and does this without ceasing to act as the Church and with no need to create a party political Christian organisation. This political service can briefly be described by referring to particular experiences which have great significance in our countries.

The first of these is the basic political formation carried out in the base Christian communities. This is not a matter of party political education but is a matter of giving the Christian people a political education so that the base communities, without ceasing to be the Church, can guide their lay people in discernment and political choice. In order to carry out this basic political education, some countries have set up specialised institutions serving the base communities. There is, for example, the Antonio Valdivieso Centre in Nicaragua or the Ecumenical Research Department in Costa Rica.

The second factor is a concerted effort to renew the social teaching of the Church. The crisis of Christian Democracy also represented a crisis for the social teaching of the Church, but today we are conscious of the need for such teaching totally separated from Christian Democracy. The social teaching of the Church needs to be freed from its Christian Democrat political captivity and to be developed in the context and spirit of the Church of the Poor. It is not enough to have a *theology* of liberation, we also need a *social teaching* of the Church. The basic element in this renewal is priority given to workers and to human life over capital, whereas previously the priority of ownership and private property was stressed. The encyclical *Laborem Exercens* of the present pope began this reworking of the social teaching of the Church in the service of the programme for liberating the poor. This social teaching will have to be much further developed in future in the light of the theology of liberation so as to meet the specific challenges coming out of the practice of the Christian people. Of course, social teaching has to be just this: *teaching*, which must in no way become economic theory or Christian political theory, still less a party political programme.

In the third place the political service rendered by the Church to the movement for liberating of the poor should seek to set up groups of people specialised in such a political service. This has become necessary where the distance between popular political parties and the Church is very great. These specialised groups need to know both the Church and the political parties well, in order to design courses of action for both churches and parties which will enable Christians to take part in the programme of liberation of the poor. In several places there are *mixed commissions* of Christians responsible for Christian communities (often theologians) and political militants set up to resolve problems related to political activity by Christians or the activity of the parties in relation to the churches.

As we have seen, when we talk of Christian political organisation we are absolutely not talking of a Christian political party or Christian political institute. What is needed is a certain organic structure that will allow Christians better to take part in the political programme of the poor, bearing these requirements in mind: that Christians who take part in party politics should do so not as a personal spontaneous affair but as part of a programme worked out and thought out by the Church; that Christians should take part in the popular movement without abandoning their Christian communities; and that the Church should provide a spirituality, pastoral approach and theology that give proper support to their political commitment; and, finally, that politically militant Christians, through their own political formation, through adequate development of the social teaching of the Church and with the help of Christian bodies specialising in the relationship between faith and politics, should provide a structured and public Christian contribution to the historical project of liberating the poor.

Translated by Paul Burns

Part II

Church and Politics

Franz Horner

The Church and Christian Democracy

1. THE CONCEPT 'CHRISTIAN DEMOCRACY'

MODERN DIALECTICAL definitions of Christian Democracy, such as that suggested by the French elder statesman and foreign minister, Georges Bidault: 'governing in the centre and, with the means of the right, carrying out the policies of the left',[1] confuse rather than clarify. An examination of the programme of the Christian Democratic parties reveals that their ideas about the content and function of Christian Democracy vary considerably from country to country. Some appeal generally and theoretically to the idea of biblical justice as their guide-line for a policy that is inspired by the Gospel. Others, on the other hand, see themselves directly as continuing, as institutionalised parties, the Social Catholicism of the late nineteenth century. As such, however, no homogeneous image emerges from a study of the history of their development. The first Christian Democratic parties, which came into being roundabout 1830 in Belgium, Ireland and France, were liberal democratic. The French and German groups had, however, to be called after 1848 conservative monarchistic, while the party that emerged in Italy towards the end of the nineteenth century displayed clear 'socialist' signs. It is therefore advisable to begin by reconstructing the history of the concept 'Christian Democracy'.

The concept has been known for centuries in England and America. The ideal of democracy is deeply rooted in Puritan faith and has concrete form in the model of the community church without any hierarchical structures. It was not by chance, but as a direct result of the Old Testament theologumenon of Samuel, who warned the Jews of the occasion of sin of placing kings over themselves, that the first notable democratic theories emerged in England.[2] It is also significant that the concept 'Christian Democracy' re-emerged in that country at the beginning of the nineteenth century, when British constitutionalism was becoming rigid. Since then, it has played a part in England in religious Socialism and in the trade unions movement. This is clear from the existence of the book *Christian Democracy*, written by the most prominent Christian Labour politician of modern England, Sir Stafford Cripps. Despite this, 'Christian Democracy' has never become a propaganda slogan of a party political movement in England or the United States. And this is not because the concept was accepted as a matter of course in an environment that simply clung to democratic ideas as the inheritance of an already secularised Christianity.

On the continent, the term *démocratie chrétienne* appeared for the first time during the French Revolution, when it had a primarily religious meaning, denoting the ideal of the democratic early Church, which, it was hoped, would be given new life by the Revolution.[3] The word acquired a greater significance between 1830 and 1848, both in Catholic Republican and in religious socialist circles, because a political dimension was added to it. By the time of the 1848 Revolution at the latest, the term was no longer used simply to denote an ideal of the Church that had to be renewed, but indicated a more just and more social order of society. It acquired a European significance only towards the end of the nineteenth century in connection with the encyclical *Rerum Novarum* of 1891, which provided the impetus for attempts, in those countries in which there had hitherto been no Christian Socialist movements, on the part of such groups to legitimate themselves by using the concept 'Christian Democracy'. In another encyclical (*Graves de Communi*), however, Leo XIII explicitly restricted the concept 'Christian Democracy' to its social and charitable content. His successor, Pius X, was even more rigorous in his opposition to all attempts to equate 'Christian social' with 'political' or even with 'democratic'.[4] The terms 'Christian Democracy', *démocratie chrétienne*, *democrazia cristiana* and so on only became finally established in continental Europe after the Second World War and then in the sense of a very large understanding of politics that embraced both the religious and social movement of the late nineteenth century and the twentieth-century Christian Democratic parties that had been emancipated from the Church.

2. THE HISTORY OF 'CHRISTIAN DEMOCRACY'

The fact that the term has a certain content and meaning today does not mean that we do not need to examine the details of the historical process in which the development of both ideas and institutions is involved. There can be no doubt that 'Christian Democracy' is constructed on a philosophical principle and the position of the political movement can also be methodically inferred from the conceptual apparatus used. All the same, the history of the ideas and that of the parties come more closely in contact with each other in the Christian parties than anywhere else, with the result that an isolated treatment of the history of the ideas and that of the organisations would not be meaningful.

If the history of effects of the movement is considered, it becomes quite clear that the contribution of the free churches to liberalism and to the working class movement or the influence of the Anglican church on Tory democracy has been far more important than efforts made by the early Christian socialists in Germany, Holland and Switzerland, which have in praxis been largely ineffectual, or those made by, for example, Lamenais in France, which were very impressive in theory.[5] Anglo-Saxon society offered no resistance to modern democracy—on the contrary, it has always regarded it as an inseparable part of religious conviction.

To put this in another way, we can say that religion and politics have developed in those countries in a kind of symbiosis. Although Church and State have always been institutionally separated in the Anglo-Saxon countries, a close spiritual relationship, which is historically based and has become, as a traditional datum that is taken for granted, the foundation of the political representative constitution, has at the same time always existed there. The typically continental European phenomenon of the Kulturkampf, to which the religious movement of 'Christian Democracy' and later even more particularly the Christian parties on the continent owe their existence, is therefore unknown both in England and in the United States.

In the Anglo-Saxon world, the model of the modern constitutional territorial State—those who come to mind above all in this context are, in addition to John Locke, the founding fathers of the United States and in particular John Adams—was conceived by the leading members of the dominant community of believers in those countries. These men insisted from the very beginning on the necessary separation of Church and State for the good of both religion and politics. On the continent of Europe, on the other hand, the secularised national State came about as the result of the revolt against the absolutism and integralism that dominated both in the Church and in the political sphere.

In this context, what above all requires an explanation is the opposition of the Catholic Church. It should not be forgotten that the reaction of Emperor Francis II to the formation of the *Rheinbund* was to lay down the German imperial crown, with the result that the disintegration of the Holy Roman Empire of the German Nation, which had already taken place *de facto* during the Napoleonic Wars, was also completed *de iure*. The Catholic Church had, because of this, lost its traditional rôle as the spiritual prop of the old imperial order.[6] The Congress of Vienna did not restore the 'Empire' in 1815, but replaced it with a system of sovereign territorial States, which had to grapple with the constitutional ideas of the French Revolution, the Napoleonic reforms and the Anglo-Saxon constitutional developments. Catholicism had to find a new orientation in a world that had been refashioned in this way and this called for a period of transition, especially as certain decisive changes had also been taking place in the internal structure of the Catholic Church between the Council of Trent and the French Revolution. From the time of the Enlightenment onwards, those in office in the Church had in particular been confronted with a powerful wave of political activity led by a bourgeoisie that had become conscious of itself in continental Europe. The question of laicism was being asked within the Church and outside it and was closely linked with the concept of 'Christian Democracy'.

To begin with, 'Christian Democracy' had a meaning that was primarily directed towards the Church. Following the example of English Puritanism, it aimed not only at political reform, but also at an inner reshaping of the Church by means of democratic structures of the community at the local level and a loosening up of the hierarchical organisation of the greater Church as a whole. The spokesmen for this *démocratie chrétienne* both before and during the French Revolution hoped that a democratised Church would have a much more radical effect on public life than a hierarchically structured community of believers. A leading representative of this new form of Catholicism[7] believed at the time that a government ought, on the basis of the Gospel, to impose legal restrictions on property and possessions, if class distinctions were to be abolished, by establishing a maximum for personal fortunes and to promote marriages between persons of different class. In order to prevent the unjustified accumulation of capital, the State ought also, it was thought, to initiate a reform of the laws of inheritance.

It is therefore possible to say that 'Christian Democracy' was *originally an attempt on the part of believers to assert themselves using political means and made possible because of the weakening of the Church's position at a time of revolution and secularisation.* If this situation is borne in mind, it is possible to understand the problems that have, since the beginning of the nineteenth century, weighed down on the relationship between the Church and democracy in continental Europe. The democratic movement has not simply been restricted to the sphere of politics and the State—it has also made a universal claim. That claim to democracy, which has been made against both the hierarchy of the Church and the absolutist monarchy, led to opposition on the part of those holding office in the Catholic Church to the idea of democracy itself. That was the situation in the Catholic countries of Europe in the nineteenth century and this explains why, despite repeated timid initiatives, it was not possible for the Christian Democratic movement to make any real political headway until the twentieth century and even then only after the Christian parties had become emancipated from the Church under the leadership of committed laymen.

Christian Democracy can therefore claim to have a relatively long tradition, not only in the purely conceptual sense, but also in fact. The majority of the Chamber of Clergy united in 1789 with the Third Estate and forced through voting by heads rather than voting by estates, an event which proved to be the death-blow to the feudal system. The 'constitutional priests' of the French Revolution, who spoke in the National Assembly of Jesus Christ as the first Democrat, soon came into conflict with the theology and praxis of the official Church. It was Lamenais who, at the beginning of the nineteenth century, not only developed an all-embracing and theologically based theory of Christian Democracy, but also began to organise the movement practically, with the result that it was able to exert some influence in the Second Republic as a liberal Catholic movement. It should, however, not be forgotten that these positive beginnings of a political movement were prevented from developing further because of the opposition of the official Church. They were in fact even consciously stifled, with all the tragic consequences within and outside of Catholic Christianity.

Despite the fact that the movement of the Christian Democrats failed after the French Revolution, the thinkers of liberal Catholicism nonetheless left traces in the nineteenth-century Church of a new awareness by conceiving models of Christian self-assertion in an environment that was gradually becoming more democratic. The Church's public position was in the future to be based not on the alliance between the throne and the altar, but on the free actions of the Church's members. Freed from the fetters of the State Church, liberal Catholicism aimed to develop the spiritual foundation of the future democratic community of States. The term 'Christian Democracy' was used with increasing frequency and there was even a little group of delegates in the French parliament who called themselves by this name. The spiritual bond that united them was great optimism with regard to the development of Democracy. In this respect, the Christian Democrats were correctly described by their contemporaries as the *parti de confiance*, the 'Party of Trust'.[8]

The heyday of 'Christian Democracy' in the nineteenth century was admittedly of short duration. It coincided with the short-lived development of the Second Republic. Because of its own interests, the official Church was no more prepared at that time to accept the idea of the sovereignty of the people and the concept of a separation of Church and State than it had been in the past. Open conflict with Rome was therefore inevitable and the Catholics who were, on their own initiative, engaged in politics were reduced to the level of outsiders in the Church. The Christian Democratic movement disappeared for some time from the field with Louis Napoleon's *coup d'état* and was replaced by the dogmatic and reactionary Syllabus Catholicism.

The Catholic social movement of the second half of the nineteenth century was not a political consequence of 'Christian Democracy' as an idea so much as a new reaction to the social and political abstinence of the *laissez-faire* liberalism that had prevailed in the economic development of the century. The Christian social movement of the late nineteenth century was characterised not by a theologically based concept of the Church, but by a decidedly emotional anti-liberalism. Its essential conviction was a rejection among Catholics of the liberals' faith that social harmony would automatically result from individual egoism.

When 'Social Catholicism' originated, a number of elements combined to play a part. Various pastoral points of view contributed to its formation and in particular the desire of the hierarchy to distance itself from the social egoism of the propertied classes and in this way to provide a counterbalance to the exodus of the working class from the Church. In addition to this, Social Catholicism was undoubtedly also a concrete expression of the sociological fact that Catholicism found itself in a proletarian minority position with regard to the 'ruling class'. This applied in the political sense above all to the formation of the Irish, Belgian and German parties in the first half of the nineteenth century. In the cultural sense and in the sphere of Church politics, it also applies to the later German 'centre' parties and to the Catholic parties in France in the Third Republic. All these parties were, in the broad sense in which Toynbee used the term, 'proletarian parties', since they represented groups in the population standing as 'enemies of the Empire' (in Prussia) or as 'ultramontane parties' (in France) outside the society legitimated by constitutional law to take part in political activity.[9] In certain Christian Democratic parties and at least in the left wing of those parties, a strong resentment against a liberal and market economy orientated policy has survived until the present time—it would not be difficult to prove this on the basis of those parties' programmes. What is particularly tragic, however, is that the working class still left the Christian community despite these efforts.

3. THE CHURCH AND 'CHRISTIAN DEMOCRACY'

If we are to understand this remarkable phenomenon, it is important to consider once again the question of the connection between the Christian Democracy of the early nineteenth century and the 'Social and Political Catholicism' and the Church of the twentieth century. As we have seen,

Christian Democracy is causally connected with Political Catholicism, as known to us from the history of the parties and indeed both movements were originally even very closely connected with each other. Common to both is the desire to reform society in the positive sense. Conceptually, however, Christian Democracy goes further than Social and Political Catholicism in certain important points. What distinguishes them from each other is the conviction that Christianity's programme of freedom can only be achieved in political democracy, because Christianity and democracy both have the same origin.[10] Christian Democracy hopes for the transformation of society, but does not expect this to come either from a strengthened form of charitable activity taking place between individuals within the framework of Catholic associations formed for this purpose or from a State social policy intervening with the aim of correcting society, but still acting within the framework of previously existing structures.[11] Christian Democracy is also not primarily concerned, as Political Catholicism was in the nineteenth and twentieth centuries, to make sure that the Church has a right to live as an unchanged hierarchically constructed structure in the modern democratic State. On the contrary, it has always hoped and expected that a renewed Church would itself become the driving force in the renewal of society. The precondition for this would be that the Church should commit itself both theologically and practically to democratic solutions.

In praxis, things were very different. After having combatted democracy for a hundred years, at the turn of the century the Church simply began to 'consume', but not to 'produce' the new freedoms. That this is not a purely subjective prejudice on my part is clear from the reality of the history of the Christian Democratic parties, although I cannot go further into this question within the scope of this article. Instead, I would once again summarise the results of analysis based on the history of ideas: From the very beginning, the words 'Christian Democracy' took on a very specific meaning that was sharply distinguished from the concepts 'Social Catholicism' and 'Political Catholicism'. In the Revolution of 1848, the term *démocratie chrétienne* in France pointed to those Catholics who, in sharp contrast to the traditionalism of de Maistre and the conservative Catholic glorification of the monarchy, were at least committed to an identification of the Church with the Republican movement, even if they did not take as their point of departure, like the Anglo-Saxon free churches, the identification of Christianity with democracy.[12] When a second *démocratie chrétienne* emerged in France, Belgium and Italy after 1891, it found itself in a similar situation. It was this term that was used to describe the tendency of those who, at the turn of the century, saw in the social message of Leo XIII not only a call to social and moral reform, but also a point of departure for the political refashioning of society. Christian

Democracy once again became a political programme 'by means of which the Catholic working class especially would be placed in a position where it would be able to take up the struggle with and continue to work with the socialist parties'.[13]

In both cases, however, the official Church distanced itself from this small vanguard of the Catholic lay movement. The first time was, after the prelude of the encyclicals *Mirari vos* (1832) and *Singulari nos* (1834) directed against liberal Catholicism, in the notorious *Syllabus* of 1864 and the second time was in Leo XIII's rather more cautious encyclical *Graves de Communi*, which was published in 1901.[14] The latter document is particularly instructive in our present reflections, because the term *Democratia Christiana* is used in it and this is the first and only time that the words 'Christian Democracy' occur in a papal encyclical. In this instance, the term, as directed against the liberal Catholic movement's understanding of itself, should be understood in the following sense: 'that every political idea is excluded and that it means no more than a charitable Christian movement for the welfare of the people'.[15] This is undoubtedly the conservative reactionary concluding point in the policy of a pope who, under certain circumstances, might have had the opportunity to bring about a decisive change in Catholicism, but who did not, however, take this step.

The social teaching of the official Church, as formulated since the end of the nineteenth century by the popes, cannot be regarded as a satisfactory contemporary social theory, because, in this official attempt at a synthesis, the insights of the modern social sciences, if they have been accepted at all, have been incorporated too late and in a contradictory manner. Even in the twentieth century, the function of papal encyclicals has to a very great extent been to save the hierarchy's medieval and integralistic claim to authority in a final protest against the change in history and against secularised and pluralistic society. Whatever attempts are made to explain the motivation, even an expert in Christian Democracy who cannot be suspected of 'laicism', such as Hans Maier, cannot help admitting that the depoliticisation of the Catholic Social movement that has been consistently carried out by the popes has, seen as a whole, had a disastrous effect on the further extension of Christian Democracy.[16] The Christian Democratic groups were never able to become large parties determining the fate of their countries for as long as the Church continued to reject democracy vehemently. Most of the Catholic parties that were founded again or reformed towards the end of the nineteenth century were set up on an altogether too narrow and politically fragmentary foundation of a pure social movement. Before 'Christian Democracy' was recognised as a political programme, many years had to pass. It was not until 1918 that the Vatican accepted modern democracy as a fact—or rather 'tolerated' it and ceased to combat it. Even then, the situation persisted until the Christmas address made by Pius XII in 1944,[17] when the official Church emerged from its previously held presuppositions and developed a more positive concept of Christian Democracy. At the same time, however, it should not be overlooked that this concept claimed to have the character of a model only for the State and not for the Church itself. It is only when the model of Christian Democracy is applied in praxis to the Church itself that the chance will exist for a renewed Church to become the driving force for a renewed society.

Translated by David Smith

Notes

1. Quoted by Hans Maier *Revolution und Kirche. Studien zur Frühgeschichte der christlichen Demokratie* 2nd enlarged edition (Freiburg 1965) p. 20.
2. Among these are, for example, the social contract theories of James Harrington and John Locke. For this, see Franz Horner 'Christliches Menschenbild—Theorem oder reale Möglichkeit gesellschaftlicher Lebensgestaltung' *Österreichische Monatshefte, Zeitschrift für Politik* 1 (1977) 18f.
3. See Hans Maier 'Herkunft und Grundlagen christlicher Demokratie' *Christliche Parteien in Europa* (Fromms Taschenbücher 31) ed. Heinz Hürten (Osnabrück 1964) p. 19f.
4. See Erika Weinzierl 'Der Antimodernismus Pius X' *Der Modernismus* ed. Erika Weinzierl (Graz, Vienna and Cologne 1974) p. 235ff., especially p. 238.
5. This is the opinion of Michael P. Fogarty in his standard work, *Christliche Demokratie in Westeuropa 1820–1953* (Basle, Freiburg and Vienna 1959) p. 8.
6. In the historical part of their contribution about Germany in the manual *Die Wahl der Parlamente und andere Staatsorgane*, edited by Dolf Sternberger and Bernhard Vogel (Berlin 1969), at p. 189, Bernhard Vogel and Rainer Olaf Schultze describe this imperial order as follows: 'The Holy Roman Empire of the German Nation was, until Emperor Francis II laid down the imperial crown on 6 August 1806, a State which was based on the estates and on the dualistic principle of division into *emperor and empire*. The estates (the nobility, the clergy and the cities with, in certain exceptional cases, the peasants) formed the basis of the assemblies, in which the whole, the *land* or the *empire* was *represented* in a corporative organisation vis-à-vis the ruler. Neither the participation of parliament in the government, which was fought for in England in the seventeenth and eighteenth centuries, nor the idea of national representation, as expressed in the French National Assembly of 1789, were ever achieved in the "old Empire" '.
7. This was the later constitutional bishop, Fouchet; see Hans Maier 'Herkunft und Grundlage der christlichen Demokratie', cited in note 3, p. 25.
8. *Ibid.* p. 29.
9. Rudolf Morsey goes more deeply into this question in his contribution on 'Die

deutschen Katholiken und der Nationalstaat zwischen Kulturkampf und Erstem Weltkrieg' in *Deutsche Parteien vor 1918* (Neue Wissenschaftliche Bibliothek 61) ed. Gerhard Ritter (Cologne 1973) especially p. 273.

10. Typical of the view that Christianity and democracy are in no way alien to each other is de Tocqueville's statement: 'Nothing in Christianity or even in Catholicism is absolutely contrary to the spirit of these societies and several things are very favourable to them'; see his *L'Ancien Régime et la Révolution*, Chapter II, *Oeuvres complètes* (Paris 1951ff.), II, p. 84, quoted in Hans Maier *Revolution und Kirche*, cited in note 1, p. 34.

11. For a long time after the Second World War it was still obvious that the political aspect was taking second place to the social aspect. Eberhard Welty, for example, devoted only a quarter of the whole text of his very representative 'Social Catechism' published in the nineteen fifties to genuinely political questions. It is also significant that, of the numerous encyclicals of Pope Leo XIII dealing with political matters, only the 'social encyclical' *Rerum Novarum* became really well known. The concept as such has persisted until the present time—this is clear from the most recent collection of papal encyclicals and other Church documents to be published: *Texte zur katholischen Soziallehre*, edited with an Introduction by Nell-Breuning, SJ and published by the Bundesverband der katholischen Arbeitnehmer-Bewegung (KAB) Deutschlands. The term 'social doctrine', however, has long fallen into disuse, because the official Church now takes up a position in its documents not only towards *social* questions, but also towards a broad spectrum of problems in *society* and of *home political* and *international* problems. Since the appearance of the encyclical *Mater et Magistra* of John XXIII at the latest, we ought therefore to speak consistently of a 'doctrine of society'.

12. The thesis that Christianity and democracy are identical was taken up again after Catholicism's decline into reactionary 'antimodernism' about the middle of our present century. For this, see the following books and articles: Jacques Maritain *Christianisme et Démocratie* (Paris 1945); *ibid. Man and State* (Chicago 1951); John Courtney Murray *Contemporary Orientations of Catholic Thought on Church and State in the Light of History* (*Theological Studies* 10, 1949), p. 177ff.; *ibid. The problem of Religious Freedom* (London 1965).

13. Hans Maier *Revolution und Kirche*, cited in note 1, p. 32.

14. It is certainly not simply a matter of chance that the encyclicals cited are not to be found in the majority of representative collections of Church documents on Catholic social doctrine, although *Graves de Communi* had the task of completing and authentically interpreting *Rerum Novarum*. The reasons why the editors of the social and ethical texts of the Catholic Church have proceeded so selectively merit detailed study.

15. Quoted from the German translation of the encyclical in the collection *Päpstliche Verlautbarungen zu Staat und Gesellschaft* (*Texte zur Forschung* 12) (Darmstadt 1973), p. 395, edited and with a commentary by Helmut Schnatz.

16. See Excursus II in Hans Maier's study of the early history of Christian Democracy, cited in note 1, p. 294ff.

17. The text of this address will be found in Helmut Schnatz, the work cited in note 15, p. 337ff.

Andrea Riccardi

The Vatican of Pius XII and the Catholic Party

1. VATICAN EUROPE AND CATHOLIC ITALY

AFTER THE second world war there was a strong revival of Christian political parties in Western Europe, and many Catholic politicians held leading positions in governments during the period of reconstruction. The socialist Auriol was able to record in his *Journal*: 'The Church has made the Triple Alliance, Adenauer, Schuman, De Gasperi, three tonsures under the same skull-cap.' There was constant talk in the press about a 'Vatican Europe'; the Catholic parties were seen as being ramifications of a unitary organisation, under the orders of the Holy See and the pope.[1] It is true that during the pontificate of Pius XII the centralising process within the Catholic church was accentuated, with a rather organic view of the activity of Catholics and of the direction of the 'Catholic world'. During recent years a number of studies have been throwing some light on the years of Pope Pacelli, showing how complex they were.[2] Nevertheless it is undeniable that, after the war, the pope sensed that the Church had arrived at a turning point in history and that it represented a civilisation, the Christian civilisation, face to face with the other, antagonistic civilisation, that of the Communist parties and the Soviet Union. But, in the context of this historic encounter, did the Catholic parties play a clearly defined part in the strategy of the Vatican of Pius XII? And did the directives emanating from the pope and from Rome help to energise and direct the formation of Catholic parties and their courses of action?

In order to reply to these questions it is necessary to give some consideration to the internal debate which troubled the Vatican during the war years and those immediately following. During this period the Holy See was living through a period of intense international isolation, its diplomacy being virtually irrelevant to the concerns of the war. Relations with the Axis powers were bad; there were none with the Soviet Union; and those with the Allied powers were cool, save for the United States of Roosevelt, with which the Holy See had good and constant relations, in which Myron Taylor played a part.[3] In this difficult situation the Vatican's diplomacy viewed with anxiety the future configuration of Europe, as it was not in agreement with the role assigned by the Americans to the USSR in Eastern Europe nor did it agree that there might be openings into the life of the Soviet Union. In reality the opinion of the Vatican was little sought on the future of Europe, except by the United States and especially about Italy, a country in which the Holy See was able to exert some influence owing to its traditional links with Rome and with the whole of Italian society.

It was in Italy that Vatican circles advanced their political ideas most clearly and decisively. For there during the war years the Church and the bishops had greatly increased their standing, which was already high during the twenty years of Fascism. Pius XII himself was very popular in Rome, as the crowded popular demonstration in St Peter's Square on 6 June 1944 showed, when the pope was acclaimed as 'defensor civitatis'. During the last part of the war the pope's popularity increased greatly in Rome itself, partly because the common people saw in him a symbol of peace, as it were in opposition to Mussolini who had willed the war.[4] But how was the great prestige of the pope and the Church in Rome and in Italy to be brought to bear on the situation? This question came under active discussion in the Vatican. It was quite clear to everyone in those circles that Italy, a nation with a traditionally Catholic religious outlook, must have nothing to do with the Soviet-controlled zone. That was a matter of vital importance to the very central organs of the Church, in Rome itself. But it might be that after the fall of the Fascist regime the Vatican thought it might exercise more influence in the country.

For Pius XII, a Roman pope, Rome, his diocese, had to be a symbolic city for the rest of the Catholic world, a laboratory of Christian civilisation, as it were. And the whole of Italy was included in this exalted idea of Rome. In the pope's view the future of Rome and of Italy was of importance to Europe and to the Catholic Church. Moreover, the men who were in a position to shape Vatican policy were all Italians—the Secretary of State cardinal Maglione, on whose death in 1944 no successor was appointed; Monsignor Tardini, Secretary for Extraordinary Ecclesiastical Affairs (the Vatican's Foreign Minister); Monsignor Montini, Substitute Secretary of State. Most of the cardinals and higher prelates in the Vatican were Italian (with a few notable exceptions, such as Cardinal Tisserant) and felt strong ties with the fate of the Holy See and that of Italy.

2. CATHOLIC PARTY, CATHOLIC PARTIES, CATHOLICS IN THE PARTIES?

A memorandum sent by the diplomat Tardini in 1943 revealed a very cautious attitude on the part of the Holy See on the question of Italy: it was proposed that there should be a strong American presence in the future of the country, and that democracy in Italy should have to go through a period of 'running in'. But throughout Europe at this time, Catholics were already taking part in the struggle for liberation and the problem of their contribution to post-war reconstruction was being secretly posed. In Italy the Christian Democratic party was already in existence, founded by an older generation deriving from the Popular Party of Father Sturzo, suppressed under Fascism, and a younger generation which had grown up in the ranks of Catholic associations during the Mussolini regime. Until a few years ago there was a hazy idea about that the Christian Democrats were the party founded because the Church wished it so. The reality is very different: The Christian Democratic party came into existence on the initiative of De Gasperi; he of course informed the Vatican, which however had little desire to be directly involved.[5]

In fact, at the close of the war the Vatican took an extremely circumspect line. This was largely due to Monsignor Tardini, responsible for the diplomatic outlook of the Secretariat of State, in a tradition going back to Cardinal Gasparri. Tardini held that the Church should avoid any direct involvement with a particular party and above all in the political struggle between the parties. Not that the prelate was hostile to the Italian Christian Democrats, but that party did not constitute a reality on which he was prepared to stake the prestige of the Church and of the pope. It would be fair to say that during an initial phase of the Vatican's attitude this diplomatic position of Tardini prevailed, although it would appear to be better adapted to situations elsewhere in Europe, for example in France. The Vatican was involved at another level, that of relations with governments, making them aware of what it saw as the priority interests of the Catholic Church.

However, the situation in Italy was a complex one: among the parties of the Resistance, alongside the Communists, the Socialists and others there was a Catholic presence, and this was represented by the Christian Democratic party. At the local level, this was bound to engage the Church in some way, if only because so many of the leading Christian Democrats were sons and daughters of the Church. Furthermore leading Christian Democrats, and foremost among them Alcide De Gasperi, got on very well indeed with Under Secretary Montini. This prelate, the son of a popular deputy, had always kept closely in touch with the Catholic associations and had virtually been the animator of some of their aspects and certain movements. He maintained close personal links with the leading figures in Catholicism and the Christian Democrats, from the old men such as De Gasperi to the young ones like Moro or Andreotti. He thought it extremely important for Catholicism to be represented in the political sphere; during the years of Fascism, Catholics had evolved a view of their own on politics and society, which they intended to apply in practice whilst accepting the challenge of democratic discussion. The suggestions of Maritain's thought, dear to Monsignor Montini, emphasise the necessity of engagement by Catholics in the sphere of politics through the concrete instrument of a political party.[6]

Hence Montini gave a great deal of encouragement to De Gasperi's Christian Democrats, whilst a whole cultural background, formed during Fascism, seemed to emphasise the role of the Catholic party as a Catholic contribution to democracy. But was the Christian Democratic party able to gain the assent of all Catholics? The fact is that ever since the closing stages of the war Catholics had been divided in their political outlook. In Rome, much was heard of a formation of young people active in the Resistance, the Christian Left, which was made up of Communist Catholics who wanted to reconcile their faith with the Marxist analysis of the class war and solidarity with the left. In the south of Italy, the sympathies of Catholics went with moderate and right wing circles; they were suspicious of the Christian Democrats, whom they judged to be too open to collaboration with the forces of the left.

At the end of the war, participation by Catholics in political life might have taken any one of a number of forms—an increased tendency to join different parties, more parties having Catholic leanings, or a single Catholic party. But a single party for Catholics would not have been an acceptable solution in France, where a strong tradition of political pluralism was deeply entrenched among Catholics, and in Italy the presence of the Communist Catholics, the strong leanings of some large groups of Catholics to the right, and the existence of the Christian Democrats, seemed to show the need for this pluralism. Would not a plurality of political outlooks among Italian Catholics have better enabled the Holy See to maintain an impartial position, distanced from the inter-party warfare, as Tardini hoped? The title of an essay by Papafave, published in 1945, translates into English as *Catholic party, Catholic parties, or Catholics in the parties?* and some members of the Vatican must have thought hard about it.

3. THE ROMAN PARTY

With the passage of time, the theoretical debate was overtaken by political events. In Italy the Christian Democratic party came to occupy a central position in political life, from 1945, when De Gasperi became president of the Council, an office which he held continuously until 1953. In the uncertainties of Vatican policy during the latter stages of the war, De Gasperi's political initiative had forced the hand of the Vatican's diplomacy and came to be a Catholic party at the centre of the Italian political spectrum. Monsignor Montini had supported this position by encouraging the Catholic Action organisations to give their support to the Christian Democrats.

However, not all the Vatican circles were in agreement with this scenario. It was not so much Tardini, whose position was well known and who continued to exert a moderating influence until the 1950's. But in the Vatican there was muffled opposition to the emergence of the Christian Democrats as a Catholic party. This opposition was strong in the curia, as well as in some groups and schools of opinion. This outlook was reflected in the pages of the Jesuit review *La Civiltà Cattolica*, an official organ of Vatican opinion. It was an area which, though not organised, was largely homogeneous, a 'Roman party' within the curia and the ecclesiastical world, with moderate, conservative political ideas, permeated by devotion to the pope and to Rome. Stronger and more coherent exponents of this group were Cardinal Ottaviani of the Holy Office and the rector of the Roman Seminary, Monsignor Ronca. To understand better the part played by the Roman party one should also bear in mind the power of the Holy Office at that time, a super-ministry among the Roman congregations, authorised to take an interest in everything connected with the defence of the integrity of the faith.[7]

The Roman party was politically hostile to the Christian Democrats. It believed their position was too much exposed to the forces of the left and not well adapted to defending Catholic interests. As the Roman party saw it, the leaders of the Christian Democrats had taken up a political and electoral stance with moderate leanings, but were constantly conducting a left of centre policy. Ottaviani and, even more, Ronco exerted pressure upon the Christian Democrats at various times to take a more moderate line. But their aims did not stop there; they wanted to offer fresh openings of a party nature to the moderate and conservative currents of opinion within the Catholic world. Their political aim was to establish a conservative party permeated by Catholicism to the right of the Christian Democrats, which would absorb part of the consensus of the latter together with right wing Catholic groupings. The Roman party was in favour of the existence of two Catholic parties, the Christian Democrats and another one of a more moderate, conservative political colour.

These circles had not been altogether pleased to see the democracy of the parties in Italy. The Popular Party of Father Sturzo, which was suppressed under Fascism, had left an unpleasing memory in many Vatican circles, because it did not beat the confessional drum and had an independent spirit which rendered it less than amenable to directives from the Holy See. Moreover, the Roman party considered that the fight against a Communist presence took precedence over every other interest; would not an excessive affirmation of democracy have weakened resistance to Communism and the USSR? This was the 'bastion' theory, defended by Cardinal Ottaviani, who held that the Church was duty bound to inspire resistance to what he called the 'Antichurch'.

Ottaviani and Ronca, the Holy Office and those of the 'Roman' persuasion, favoured pluralism of politics and parties among Catholics, in order to build up an alternative to De Gasperi's Christian Democrats. Even vis-a-vis the Communist Catholics, the Holy Office adopted a softer attitude than did Montini, not so much because it was sympathetic to their political ideology as because the presence of a small Catholic party of the left would have legitimised the existence of a larger Catholic party to the right of the Christian Democrats. But it was not long before the Communist Catholics were condemned by the Holy See—it is thought that the Christian Democrats made representations at this level—and they were dissolved in 1945.

4. A SINGLE PARTY OF CATHOLICS

Tardini seemed embarrassed by a too unequivocal involvement of the Church with a political party; the Roman party was definitely hostile to the strength of the Christian Democrats in the Catholic world. So how was it that the Christian Democrats were able to emerge as the only party of Italian Catholics? Moreover in Belgium, Holland and West Germany too, the bishops ended up by supporting Catholic unity in the political sphere in the post-war period. In Germany the bishops supported the CDU, even if somewhat hesitantly; the CDU-CSU are not a Catholic party like the old Centre party. The Jesuit Zeiger, in a report he wrote on German Catholics and politics, concluded by stating that there was no longer a veritable Catholic party in Germany. The Dutch bishops discouraged labour-oriented initiatives, whilst Cardinal Van Roey condemned the political divisions between Catholics (he said in 1945 that it was a baneful error for Catholics to 'be dissipated across the political spectrum'). In France, despite the existence of MRP, a party influenced by Catholicism, Catholic voters were divided and pluralist, with Catholic votes going to the Gaullist party as well. The situation in Europe is complex and diversified, even though Catholics, with the notable exception of France because of its very strong pluralist tradition, tend to concentrate their votes on one party, encouraged to do so by the hierarchy itself.

In the Italian situation this came about by a decision on the part of the Holy See, which increasingly saw in the Christian Democrats the only party which could effectively counter the influence of Socialism and Communism. Nevertheless there was no lack of hostility towards the Christian Democrats; there were many in the Vatican who attacked it for pursuing policies too much inclined to the centre-left, too attentive to the susceptibilities of its allies in government and little inclined to heed the voice of the Church. This state of mind as regards the Christian Democrats started at the Liberation and lasted until the 1950's. Pius XII himself fully shared the critical attitude towards the Christian Democrats; in interviews he did not always evince agreement with De Gasperi's actions—indeed there was at times real tension between the two.[8] However, the pope was too apprehensive that any break might harm the resistance of Catholics to the parties of the left after the 1946 elections.

The theme of a single party was openly supported in the Vatican by Under Secretary Montini, who saw in it both a means of coherently translating a Christian project into political action and also a way to give Italian Catholics a firm commitment to the democratic process. With Catholics united in a single party it would have been impossible for groups of Italian Catholics to drift towards the right into positions not compatible with the values of democracy. Pius XII appeared to be less conscious than Monsignor Montini of the urgency of committing Italian Catholics to the path of democracy through the Christian Democrats. But Montini was also able to present the Christian Democrats as the only united endeavour of Italian Catholics to face up to the left; this was deeply congenial to the pope's views, and he did not hesitate to place his own authority behind them in the elections.

What this means is that Montini's views prevailed over those of the Roman party and the caution of Tardini. But the victory of this contention depended on the direct will of the pope. In 1945 *La Civiltà Cattolica* came out in favour of unity among Italian Catholics, even though theoretically envisaging plurality of parties: 'Catholics can in normal circumstances form parties' wrote that authoritative reiew in 1946. But could post-war Italy be described as 'normal circumstances'? The emergency arose from the confrontation with the forces of the left. As long as the emergency of this encounter lasted, the pope always gave higher priority to Catholic unity than to any other problem. But as the years passed, the Roman party in various ways toyed with scenarios involving the splitting of the Christian Democrats; a second Catholic party was a standing and barely concealed threat to the political action of De Gasperi, who was very sensitive to the problem of ecclesiastical and Catholic consensus.

5. CHURCH PARTY OR SECULAR PARTY?

The crisis in the Popular Party had been caused by its abandonment by the Church, which had been pursuing a policy of attempting to reach a *modus vivendi* with the Fascist regime, an endeavour consummated in the Lateran Pact of 1929. De Gasperi, who had lived through those events, was well aware of the value of the political support that the Church could give to a Catholic party in Italy. He never lost sight of that problem. Besides, in Italy the prime motive force of the Christian Democrats was provided by the Catholic world. It was that world with its organisations—primarily Catholic Action—with the hierarchy, that gave strong support to the party in the general elections. The elections held on 18 April 1948, the first to be held after the proclamation of the Republic, have remained in the popular memory as an occasion on which huge support for the Christian Democrats was mobilised by Catholics.

The support of the Church and of Catholic organisations was vitally important to the Christian Democrats.[9] And the Holy See intended that support to influence political decisions as well. Pius XII, the Roman party and Vatican circles demanded from the Christian Democrat political class constant obedience to the directives of the Holy See: to strengthen the anti-communist commitment, to safeguard Catholic interests, to prevent anticlerical demonstrations, and so on. One organisational view of the Catholic bloc saw the Christian Democrats as a transmission belt for the will of the Church in the political sphere, like other Catholic organisations in other spheres. This outlook, though expressed schematically, was in line with the thinking of Pius XII and of the Catholic organisations which were thrown into the electoral contest in support of the Church party against the 'Antichurch'.

This was not what De Gasperi had in mind. But neither was it Monsignor Montini's idea, for, although he had decided to support the theme of one party for Catholics, he did not look upon the party as one of the expressions of the Catholic bloc. Backing up De Gasperi, Montini wanted to confirm the autonomy of the Catholic political governing class, to which the Church should delegate all responsibility for managing political relationships. In brief, both Montini and De Gasperi saw the Christian Democrats as a party of the Catholics, supported by the Church but also a political force with a Christian background, able to make its own choices and develop its own strategies in political and parliamentary life. Within this framework, Montini and De Gasperi tended to limit the role of Gedda and of Catholic Action in the political field, entrusting to the association primarily a training role. By contrast, the Roman party saw in Gedda, president of the association, a figure capable of shaking De Gasperi's unchallenged leadership.

Something that De Gasperi said at the National Council of the Christian

Democrats in 1954 about the party's secularity as a political party seems like a confession of the intellectual course he had followed until then. The Vatican circles were much displeased with the elder statesman's speech, so much so that at the direct request of the pope *La Civiltà Cattolica* had printed a very direct contradiction of the arguments of the Christian Democrat leader on the subject of secularity. This episode, which occurred just before De Gasperi's death, expressed the tension that existed throughout the years of reconstruction between the Vatican—including the pope—and the Christian Democrats in Italy. Very many in the Vatican looked upon the Christian Democrats as the party of the Church, sustained by the Church and morally bound to adhere more closely to the policies of the Catholic bloc.[10] Both the pope and the Roman party made such demands, and on several occasions the latter pressed for the title of Catholic party to be withdrawn from the Christian Democrats. On the other hand, however, Under Secretary Montini saw to it that the services rendered by the Christian Democrats from 1945 onwards in defence of the Church and in the struggle against the communists did not go unremarked. In a certain sense, some ecclesiastical circles including Ottaviani, Ronca and others, regarded Monsignor Montini as the main obstacle to making their own influence and demands felt in the Catholic party. But after the end of the war it was precisely Montini's office, that of Under Secretary at the Secretariat of State, which came to have the decisive voice on political and religious matters in Italy.

6. SPANISH MODEL OR DEMOCRATIC MODEL

In considering the rebuilding of democracy in Italy and other European countries we have to ask ourselves what political model was in the minds of the Vatican of Pius XII. It is true that the alliance of Fascism with Nazism (followed by Italy's entrance into the war) had put an end to the dream of catholicising Mussolini's regime, which was cherished in some Catholic quarters after the Lateran Pacts. When the war ended and the transition from Fascism to democracy began, some circles in the Vatican entertained thoughts of a certain part that could be played by Italian soldiers in a kind of Catholic-military regime. But, as is clear from Tardini's attitudes and from the correspondence with the United States, the Holy See had no intention of allowing its great authority to be dissipated in such experiments. It viewed democracy as a critical choice which must be made, and the Vatican did not wish to withdraw Catholics from that choice. Moreover, during the war years Pius XII had made it clear under his pontificate that 'if the future belongs to democracy, an essential part of its fulfilment must devolve upon the religion of

Christ and the Church', as he said in a radio broadcast at Christmas 1944. Besides the acceptance of democracy and opposition to 'monopoly of a dictatorial power ... incompatible with the dignity and the liberty of citizens', the pope also had a strong conviction of the part he and the Church were called to play in proclaiming the value of human beings, natural law and the Christian message. Hence in Pius XII an emphasis on the role of the Church as the 'mistress of civilisation' was coupled with an unequivocal acceptance of the democratic system.

Catholic parties, also obeying the unchanging teaching of the pope, acted in accordance with those principles, even though the policies they pursued vary greatly in different countries.[11] The protagonists of Catholicism shared a vision of civilisation to be carried into political and community life. This outlook was the basis on which specific political programmes were worked out, then subjected to the severe test of the realities of economic and social events in the aftermath of the second world war. However, the pope's teaching also emphasised the central role of the Church—not only that of Catholics— in democratic society; but how can this be implemented in a pluralist system in which other political forces with secular, Socialist, Communist, Conservative and other traditions are also present? *La Civiltà Cattolica* speaks of a role of the Church as the 'queen of society'. But such a position does not always appear to be compatible with the realities of a pluralist democracy.

In fact, under this system the Church is placed on the same level as the other forces impinging on society and political life, whilst the press and public opinion are quite free to criticise, sometimes carrying their attacks to the verge of anticlericalism. The reactions of Vatican circles to this climate, which became extremely fierce during the hard conflict with the Communists and Socialists, were very strong. Pope Pius XII himself made many public and private complaints to members of the Italian government and the leaders of the Christian Democrats with regard to affairs in Rome and Italy. It is clear that these difficulties arose in Italy, after 1946 and above all after 1948, when the electoral success of the Christian Democrats reached its zenith. This climate was also worsened by the hard line taken by the Vatican with respect to the Communist presence in Italy. Both Vatican circles and Pope Pius XII himself claimed that the policy of the Christian Democrats in Italy against the Communists and Socialists appeared to be too weak, after the excommunication of 1949 and after the openly anti-religious demonstration represented by policies towards the Church followed in the countries of Eastern Europe. The pope held that it was a priority concern of the Catholic party to contain the Communists.

In this difficult atmosphere, the moderates within the Vatican, the Roman party and even Cardinal Ottaviani once again put forward a proposal for a

State that was not exactly modelled on modern democracy—the Catholic State, similar to that ruled by Franco in Spain, in which only the 'truth' has the right to freedom, error being allowed at most the chance of toleration. And the Socialists and Communists, thus formally condemned by the Church, basically represented 'error'.[12] Thus 'error' became incorporate in the Socialist and Communist parties, against which a Catholic State was to take severe measures (as, incidentally, were called for in Italy against the existence and the propaganda of some Protestant groups). But was Italy really a Catholic State? After 18 April 1948, with the decisive victory of the Christian Democrats, moderates within the Vatican wondered why a regime more obviously aligned with the Catholic blueprint was not set up in the country. But the truth was that only in the Iberian peninsula did States on the 'Catholic pattern' really exist.

In fact, *La Civiltà Cattolica*, the Jesuit review very close to the Roman party, frequently carried expressions of appreciation of the Spanish regime and did not conceal its distaste for the Anglo-Saxon type of democracy. Father Messineo wrote that the Franco regime 'as regards non-catholic cults is broadly, even if not entirely, in line with the doctrine of the Church'. And it was Catholic and Francoist circles in Spain that suggested to the Vatican, just before the elections of 18 April 1948, taking steps with the help of the Americans to bar the Communists by law from presenting candidates at the elections. However, Pius XII gave a clear reply to this suggestion, which would have turned Italy into a country similar to Spain. He said: 'To take such action would encourage a revolution and would be inconceivable in the light of democratic procedures.' The pope was fully aware that such authoritarian undertakings were too hazardous.

Nevertheless, those in the Vatican had considerable difficulty in accepting fully fledged democratic pluralism. The danger of a Communist victory was held out, and the lack of respect by public opinion for the Church and its ministers was cited. There was a certain coolness towards the Spanish pattern, as for example in circles close to Monsignor Montini, whilst even Tardini was not specially enamoured of Franco. But others—Ottaviani among them—viewed Spain as an example to be praised and recommended in Europe and, above all, in Latin America. In 1952, for instance, the cardinal made a public speech in which he praised a State modelled on the Spanish pattern. This initiative may perhaps be seen as part of the pressure that was exerted for the conclusion of a concordat between the Holy See and Spain, about which Pius XII hesitated for a long time, as did the Secretariat of State. The concordat was signed in 1953, shortly before the agreements between Spain and the United States, and constituted a significant diplomatic and moral success for Franco.

7. DEMOCRACY AND A CATHOLIC PARTY

From the end of the war until the conclusion of the pontificate of Pius XII, some important personages in the Vatican were extremely displeased with the Christian Democrats because of the failure of the party to reduce the extent of Communist penetration of Italian society and its reluctance to make the State more Catholic. What these malcontents had in mind was Franco's Spain. Nevertheless, the anti-De Gasperi party was in the main defeated and the Christian Democrats forged ahead as the only party of the Catholics in Italy, with a central position in the political spectrum and in governments of the Republic. This party, which came into being through the will of De Gasperi and with the support of Montini, was before long well established and difficult to disavow. Pius XII, who to some extent shared moderate criticism of the party, was well aware that nothing could take its place and that no good purpose would be served by destabilising it, because it formed a bulwark against the Communists. With the passing of time, thoughts of creating alternative Conservative groupings to the Christian Democrats, possibly making use of support from the right, gradually faded away. Parties have a life of their own in Italian society, and the Christian Democrats too came to depend structurally less and less on the Church, even though her support was valuable.[13]

Thenceforward the only matter in dispute between the Vatican and the Christian Democrats was the party's independence of directives from the Vatican. For example, when municipal elections were held in Rome in 1952, Pius XII wanted the Catholic party to make common cause with the parties of the right in order to hold back the Communists. This, however, would have been a reversal of the centrist policy conducted by De Gasperi. This operation (which has been called 'operation Sturzo') was rejected by the Christian Democrat leader, who thereupon was reproved by the pope. That was just one of many national or local episodes in which disputes arose between the Church and the Christian Democrats concerning the freedom of political action allowed to the party. Then from the end of the 1950's until the 1960's an energetic debate arose between the Church and the Christian Democrats with reference to a new relationship with the socialist party. This was the so-called 'opening to the left' advocated by Moro and Fanfani, which caused heartsearchings among many Italian bishops. But while this was going on, Pius XII died and John XXIII became pope.

That is how the single party of Catholics, the Christian Democratic party, became established in Italy. Clearly, this fact diminishes political pluralism among Catholics. But perhaps, from a practical viewpoint, it prevents the Catholic vote from edging towards parties of the right (and it should be remembered that the Catholic world, having experienced Fascism, tended towards a moderate outlook). When elections are called, ecclesiastical authority publicly rallies around the Christian Democrats, even if privately it regrets that the Catholic leaders of the party take too little notice of the counsels of the Church in making their political choices. Nevertheless there can be no doubt that in the early years of the Republic the Church made a vital contribution to the successful buildup of the Christian Democratic party.

Can the scenario of a single party for Catholics, strictly incorporated in the Christian Democrats, be exported to other countries? In France, the situation is very different. When in 1951 the *Osservatore Romano* advised Catholics in France to vote MRP, it being a Catholic party, the call was coldly received by the French episcopate and evoked sharp ripostes from French politicians.[14] The fact is that, unlike Italy and other places in Europe, democratic pluralism in France has no experience of a single party for Catholics. Elsewhere in Europe, when the Churches decide to support the party with a Christian background the impetus comes less from Rome than from the will and guidance of the national episcopates. In Italy, the bishops play no part in political affairs. The directives come from the Secretariat of State, from the Vatican, even from the pope himself. In fact, until the Council the Holy See was the only coordinating centre that existed in the Church in Italy.[15]

Hence the political situation in Italy after the second world war constituted a laboratory in which the various opinions that existed in the world of the Vatican were projected, without the intermediary and responsibility of a national episcopate. The result is that the high functionaries in the Vatican are much involved in policy in Italy, and nearly all of them are of Italian origin. Thus Italy was a laboratory for originating a Catholic party, in which the directives of the Holy See could be tried out after having been matured in discussion and contention behind the discreet walls of the Vatican. Seldom do echoes of this discussion and contention reach the outside world, as when Monsignor Montini was transferred to Milan as archbishop in 1954. Nevertheless, conflict exists. In this situation many directives are matured which in part are also sent to countries other than Italy, countries more distant and less receptive, where the hold of the Holy See is less secure and direct. So the Italian experience in the post war years is very individual and, some would say, very 'Vatican'. But it is still extremely significant that since 1945 the Church and large masses of Catholic people have been actively involved, through the experiment of the Catholic party, in building democracy. The words of De Gasperi, spoken in 1952, give some hint of the travail entailed by involving the Catholic world in democracy: 'Should not even we be worried, we who lean for support on the Catholics, so amenable to dictatorial government and to Conservative ideas? ... in the light of Catholic history, we are not justified in asking people to take it for granted that we stand for freedom. Catholics have always been divided on this point.' So said the Italian statesman.

Translated by Alan Braley

Notes

1. On this subject see J. M. Mayeur *Des Partis catholiques à la Démocratie chrétienne* (Paris 1980), and *idem.* 'Pio XII e i movimenti cattolici in Europa' in *Pio XII*, ed. A. Riccardi (Bari 1984) pp. 277–293.

2. See *Pio XII*, ed. A. Riccardi, especially the historiographical essay by F. Traniello *Pio XII dal mito alla storia*, pp. 5, 29.

3. See E. Di Nolfo *Vaticano e Stati Uniti, 1939-1952* (Milan 1978). See also P. Pastorelli 'Pio XII e la politica internazionale' in *Pio XII*, cited in note 1, at pp. 125–147.

4. A. Riccardi *Roma 'città sacra'? Dalla Conciliazione all'operazione Sturzo* (Milan 1976).

5. This hypothesis, largely substantiated by subsequent research, was advanced by P. Scoppola *La proposta politica di De Gasperi* (Bologna 1977).

6. On government checks and balances during the time of Pius XII, see A. Riccardi 'Governo e "profezia" nel pontificato di Pio XII' in *Pio XII*, the work cited in note 1, at pp. 31-92. The records of a colloquium held at the Ecole française di Roma on Paul VI and modernity, (Rome 1984) are of special interest; see in particular R. A. Graham 'G. B. Montini Substitute Secretary of State' (in tandem with Domenico Tardini), in the work cited in note 1, at pp. 66, 82. Cardinal Tardini threw an original light on the years of Pius XII in an address given on the first anniversary of the death of that pope, *Pius XII* (Vatican City 1960).

7. See A. Riccardi *Il 'partito romano' nel secondo dopoguerra (1945–1954)* (Brescia 1982) which endeavours to trace a geography of this group and to identify its policy. Obviously this grouping, since it was an ecclesiastical lobby, did not have an official name of its own, but was a polycentric reality made up of affinities of outlook and a wide variety of sub-groups.

8. On this Italian statesman, see also the memoirs of G. Andreotti who worked with him: *De Gasperi visto da vicino* (Milan 1986).

9. There is by now a large bibliography on the Catholic political class of the post-war era, after more than ten years of discussion and controversy. See, *inter alia*, A. Giovagnoli *Le premesse della ricostruzione* (Milan 1982) which examines the relationship between the political engagement and the different types of spirituality of the Catholic leaders; R. Moro *La formazione della classe dirigente cattolica (1929–1937)* (Bologna 1979), with an analysis of the period of preparation under Fascism.

10. On the Italian Christian Democrats, see a large and representative work by G. Baget-Bozzo *Il partito cristiano al potere* (2 vols., Florence 1974).

11. An interpretation of the experience in Germany and in Italy is presented in *Konrad Adenauer e Alcide De Gasperi; due esperienze di rifondazione della democrazia*, ed. U. Corsini and K. Repgen (Bologna 1984). See also C. Brezzi *I partiti democratici cristiani d'Europa* (Milan 1979).

12. G. Hermet *Les Catholiques dans l'Espagne franquiste* (2 vols., Paris 1980).

13. Some remarks on the period of the so-called catholic hegemony in Italy, in P. Scoppola *La 'nuova cristianita' perduta* (Rome 1985). See also G. Alberigo 'Santa Sede e vescovi nello Stato unitario. Verso un episcopato Italiano (1958–1985)' in *Storia d'Italia, Annali 9, La Chiesa e il potere politico*, (Turin 1986).

14. See R. Rémond 'Forces religieuses et partis politiques', in *Forces religieuses et attitudes politiques*, ed. R. Remond (Paris 1965) pp. 57–87.

15. See A. Riccardi 'Chiesa di Pio XII o Chiesa italiana?' in *Le Chiese di Pio XII* ed. A. Riccardi (Bari 1986).

Part III

Particular Cases

Walter Dirks

Reflections from Germany

OCCASIONALLY GERMAN democrats have remembered that the pre-Christian Germanic world contained not only authoritarian—the title 'Herzog' (=duke) derives from the tribal and martial leaders—but 'democratic', that is, independent, structures. They did not prove historically effective. When the Germanic tribes settled down after the great migration, they were integrated into the dual system which, in Eastern as in Western Europe, was ordained, on the one hand, by Roman imperial power and, on the other hand, by the hierarchical constitution of the Church, and later, at the peak of the medieval period, by the structure represented by the supreme authorities of Emperor and Pope. There were various 'democratic' structures in the cities in so far as artisans were able to assert themselves in contradistinction to feudal and patrician groups, but they were as ineffectual on a large scale as the first attempts at peasant liberation.

In the Reformation period there was an opportunity for a union of towns and peasants against nobles and princes that would have produced a different result. Nevertheless, the liquidation of the medieval system under the Reformation was restricted to the dimension of inwardness. The hegemony of the uniform authoritarian system was maintained, and as it fragmented the Empire split first into the German principalities, and outside the country into national States. It was disastrous for the German consciousness that Germany became a national State only much later, in the second half of the nineteenth century, and did so under the leadership of the most powerful monarch, the King of Prussia. Even though the French Revolution had been a mighty inspiration for the German bourgeoisie across the Rhine, and for half a century, between 1806 and 1849 approximately, the idea of liberty had been intimately associated with that of unity, in 1871 that same German bourgeoisie accepted Bismarck's offer of unity—but only at the price of abandoning the search for liberal democracy.

1. EVEN IN THE NINETEENTH CENTURY ...

In general German Catholics followed this process, but tardily. The Romantics, who rediscovered the middle ages after the great period of German classic literature, seemed for a time to offer Catholics the possibility of national integration. But when the bourgeois affected by the middle-class revolution in France articulated their will to freedom, Catholics took up the new watchword mainly in a typically variant form. The Catholic organisations formed after the unsuccessful democratic venture at the Paulskirche asked above all for freedom to obey the pope. They saw themselves as national 'too', but their counter-reformation ecclesiality gave them an orientation different to that of the majority of the nation. The state of defensive Kulturkampf led to a demarcation from the liberal and against the Protestant culture of the century. The constitutional monarchy (in which Parliament restrained the sovereignty of monarchical and oligarchical rule only to some extent, mainly through the right to pass the budget for the individual states), seemed to spur Catholics to enter the political arena. They did so in order to have some influence on broader politics and to organise themselves as the Catholic party. To be sure, by reason of its federalism and cultural conservatism, the 'Centre Party' also attracted Protestants, but only to a limited degree.

The active Catholics, whether they were now otherwise of a conservative or of a progressive bent or mind, and whether they were middle-class, peasants or aristocrats, in party-political terms contributed only their Catholicity to parliament; therefore their party had a clearly delineated profile only in terms of cultural policy. This (the sole) party representing a religion or philosophy of life was not in fact a cogent democratic structure. In a sense, its opponents could justly reproach the Catholics and their party for 'ultramontanism'. Essentially, so it seemed, they thought and acted not within the social union of the nation, but under the control of the ecclesial HQ in Rome.

When Bismarck at that very time declared that Catholics and Socialists were enemies of the national and monarchical Empire, it might have been possible to have formed a democratic opposition together with the Socialists. But since Rome condemned not only liberalism but Socialism (most emphatically in Leo XIII's encyclical *Rerum novarum*), partly for religious polemical reasons and partly out of adherence to a conservative and hierarchical social order, this opportunity was missed. The formula 'throne and altar' remained dominant, certainly in the Catholic states and provinces of the Empire, though Protestants too could count on the loyalty of Catholics. But the Catholic nobility, who played a considerable role in Catholicism, especially in the Rhineland and in Silesia, were certainly involved in an aristocratic cartel, so to speak, with the kings and princes. (The question of the extent to which the bishops saw themselves as princes of the Church and in a feudal sense as appertaining to the nobility, or rather as close to the people, deserves special study).

In the Centre Party, Catholicism was able to express social but not liberal-democratic impulses. Therefore the attitude of the German Church in the nineteenth century and in the decade of the twentieth century before the first world war was largely determined by circumstances, above all by the delicate situation of the German Church poised between national loyalties and those of the Roman counter-reformation system.

2. AFTER THE FIRST WORLD WAR

After the reversals of the first world war, Catholicism and the Centre allowed the revolution (no revolution, in fact) to occur passively. Yet the 1919 constitution afforded a new situation. The suspect revolutionary movement had become consolidated as a democratic order. Now the Reichstag was the democratic sovereign responsible for all political decisions. In this situation it would have been possible for German Catholics to see themselves as productively distant from all parties. That would have given them the opportunity to introduce Christian commitment into all progressive parties in accordance with the Gospel formula of the salt and the leaven. But they remained attached to the Centre which they had inherited. A second possibility, advocated by Joseph Wirth and his friends, would have been to define the Centre Party itself no longer denominationally but politically. Then it would have been possible, together with the Social Democrats and the radical democratic middle class, to have supported with a political programme the establishment of the social and democratic republic proclaimed in the 1919 constitution. But this possibility, too, came to nothing.

The Party defined itself as 'Centre', yet did not fill this centre with real political contents, but became and remained a function of left and of right. And so it neutralised itself, and furthermore was represented in all regimes: in the left-wing and later in the right-wing government. The party chairman, Wilhelm Marx, defined the Centre as a 'constitutional party', one which could accommodate monarchists just as easily as republicans and democrats; he might also have said: as easily as nationalists and pacifists. Its neutrality deprived the party of its democratic function, to the cost of the Republic and of German Catholicism.

Hence it also proved lacking in face of the Fascist threat which was becoming obvious in 1930. Like the other bourgeois and proletarian forces, it opposed only the satanic Adolf Hitler and his anti-Christian populist movement, but did not see that that movement's real opportunity was to be found only in the gathering union forged by the National Socialists with the army, the civil service, the law, and the major industrialists.

German Catholicism had learnt nothing from Marxism. It did not think historically or in terms of political forces. It interpreted political action (like all moral activity) in neo-scholastic and casuistical terms on the basis of an inherited complex of norms; it did not acknowledge such fundamental political categories as decision and risk. Therefore German Catholicism, which had committed itself so unequivocally against National Socialism on a moral plane, remained without any recourse in the face of the Fascist threat. It was taken unawares by the victory of the union of right-wing forces. In the last years before Hitler's 'assumption of power' an anti-Fascist united front against dictatorship would have been only too apt, and the Catholics, the Centre and the Catholic organisations would necessarily have comprised a major component of such a front. Not only the Communists, the Social Democrats and the democratic element among the middle class, but the spokesmen of political Catholicism were responsible for the lack of such a united front.

3. AFTER THE SECOND WORLD WAR

Catholicism's inadequacy to that end proved an unhealthy legacy after the war and with the end of totalitarian rule. The restoration began as early as spring 1945, when one by one the proletarian and middle-class parties which had collapsed in 1933 revived. The Christian Democratic Union (the Christian Social Union in Bavaria) established itself as in certain respects a new form of party, in view of the growing ecumenical conciliation of the various denominations. But to a considerable extent, the party harked back to the Centre of the Weimar period. It was not the small Centre Party, which still exists today in a few areas, but the Union which was Centre's heir. We may assume that all the Centre voters of the Weimar period, whose number remained happily constant up to the last free election of March 1933 independently of other fluctuations in electoral behaviour, came together again in the CDU. The additional Protestants, however, were recruited not so much from among the supporters of the Confessing Church, who, with or without the mediation of Gustav Heinemann's 'All-German People's Party', went over to the Social Democrats, as from the reservoir of the two other formations in Protestantism in the Hitler period. They came from the (Nazi) German Christians and the largely Lutheran supporters of middle-class nationalism. That considerably strengthened the party's conservative tendency.

The history of 'Christian Democracy' in West Germany since the end of the last war as summarised above has to be distinguished wholly from the history of the equivalent parties in Italy, France, Latin America and elsewhere in the world. It will be asked whether and to what extent the German solution, which certainly had an inspirational effect in Italy and in France, also became a model for the Christian Democratic parties in South and Central America.

There are three Christian Democratic parties in the territory of the former German Empire. I shall say nothing about the CDU in the German Democratic Republic (East Germany), which exists under the very special conditions of that largely Communist State. The 'Christian Social Union' in the 'Bavarian Free State', the successor to the 'Bavarian People's Party' of the Weimar period, which similarly existed alongside the non-Bavarian Catholic party, is to a considerable degree more conservative (or more reactionary too) than the larger sister party. The Catholic element in it is also more pronounced than in the CDU, which especially in North Germany is affected by its minority (and in some areas, majority) of Protestants. Considering that the Bavarian party chose the term 'social' instead of 'democratic', there is certainly less of an acknowledgment of the social dimension. This is clearly a reflection of the old Catholic disinclination for democracy inherited from the nineteenth century. The CSU forms a common bloc with the CDU in parliament, and belongs to the context of this article.

The origin of the CDU cannot be understood apart from the ecumenical impulse. After the dictatorship which acted repressively towards both denominations, it seemed obvious that Catholics and Protestants should come together in the new form of State. That also meant a common demarcation from both socialist parties and from political liberalism. In terms both of the party leaders and of its members and electors, then, the CDU became a decidedly bourgeois and landed-farmer party. In the Centre tradition, it had a considerable workers' component, which however was unable to exploit its dual position, as an employees' group in the CDU, and as a Christian group in the trade unions, for purposes of decisive commitment in the Federal Parliament and in the German Trade Union Congress. In spite of this wing, the CDU remained a bourgeois party.

For that reason alone, but also in respect of its options, the CDU may be categorised as the party of the *status quo*, for which the future is essentially an extension of the present. That has been especially true in the last few years, and to an increasing degree. There is an exception to this tendency: within the CDU conservatism is directed no longer against technological progress but includes it. (Franz Josef Strass and Lothar Späth, the leaders of the Bavarian CSU and CDU in Baden-Württemberg, particularly emphasise new technologies and the technological efficiency of the Union). Nevertheless, the Union may be classified as the conservative people's party which has to look for its members and electors at levels where people are interested in the maintenance of their professional life and their assets.

Because of these facts alone, the Christian nature of the Union has to be called in question. Christians who for whatever motives are always critically opposed to the ruling, socially cautious Capitalist system necessarily contest the legitimacy of the letter 'C' in CDU or CSU. It is only appropriate that the Union does not include most of those Catholics who in the spirit of Vatican II are committed to Church renewal, in accordance with the wishes of Pope John XXIII: along the clear lines of the primitive Church and the 'aggiornamento', and in productive engagement with the present day. This applies to Christians who wish to take seriously the splendid solidarity of the Church as proclaimed in the introductory statement of the constitution *Gaudium et spes*. The political left in German Catholicism is accordingly largely identical with the renewal movement within the Church.

The party ideology accords with this state of affairs. In so far as it ever defines tasks and goals determined by Christian commitment, the normative-casuistical attitude of Catholic social teaching applies, but without any development in the direction of 'labourism', an agreement that labour takes precedence over capital. Inasmuch as it is content with a limited reform of the existing society, it does not face up to the new threats which make it necessary to work for 'another republic', 'another Europe' and another world order. Unlike the 'theology of liberation' it avoids the category of history under way, of history which has to be worked out meaningfully. It thinks in terms of principles and norms, not social structures, and not the category of historical risk. It does not acknowledge the significance of existing political forces which anyone concerned with social change has to take into account. Therefore it does not realise that productive and curative solutions of our existential problems can be found only if the progressive forces which have become effective in European history, the forces of Christianity, of the socialist working-class movement, and of the radical-democratic minority of the liberal middle class, unite in consensus, strategy and action against actively or passively reactionary and repressive forces and structures, and thus against 'wolves', parasites and the indifferent.

We may derive the spiritual position contrary to those who illegitimately claim to be a party of Christians from Jesus's remarks about salt and leaven. The committed Christians of the Federal Republic must take part above all as active minorities in all productive organisations, and principally in the SPD, CDU and among radical democratic citizens.

What is the attitude of the official churches to the above situation? Whereas the Protestant churches of the various *Länder* and the Evangelical Church in Germany have maintained and maintain a certain equal distance from the established parties and from the Greens, the German bishops attempted this kind of 'equal distance' for only a short time. In the first years of the Federal Republic the prominent figure of Konrad Adenauer, whom most Catholics and certainly most bishops saw as the politician whom God had sent to the poor Germans, defined the identity of Church and party. Whether Cardinal Frings depended more on Adenauer or Adenauer more on Frings is an open question. Even today this kind of identity is often met with in the fatal uncertainty experienced in face of the statement that 'we' have to do this or that. Then it sometimes has to be asked who exactly this 'we' refers to—we Catholics or we CDU supporters? In pastoral letters the bishops have always exhorted their flocks to vote 'appropriately'—never directly and expressly, but all the more unequivocally indirectly. Recently, moreover, there has been no more talk of equidistance.

Since the Constantinian turning-point, the identity as outlined above of the Catholic Church and of the party of Christian democracy has derived from ancient history, from, in fact, the dual system of empire and Church in the Middle Ages and from its secularised form as a 'Christian civilization'. Whatever the situation of Christian-Democratic groups in other countries may be, in West Germany the alliance of the two Union parties cannot be seen as the historically appropriate answer to the question of what political commitment requires of the Catholic Church and its office, and of what it demands of Catholic and Protestant Christians. The claim of the Union parties to be the political formation of Christians contradicts both the democratic rules of the game and the critical and prophetic claim of Christianity.

Translated by J. G. Cumming

Daniele Menozzi

The Case of Italy

1. ORIGINS OF THE EXPRESSION 'CHRISTIAN DEMOCRACY'

THE TERM and the concept of Christian Democracy, which arose during the French Revolution—probably from A. Lamourette, constitutional bishop of Lyons, who used it in his speech to the National Legislative Assembly in 1791—also made its first appearance in Italy during the Jacobin triennium (1797–99). Clergy and laity in various parts of the peninsula—Liguria, Emilia, Marche, Rome—called themselves Christian Democrats meaning they wanted political and religious reforms, not necessarily always the same ones. They were united in their effort to reconcile Catholicism with the principles of 1789 and in particular in wanting to show that the Church was not against a regime based on the sovereignty of the people. They wanted political changes to be accompanied by a renewal in Church government: in some cases they insisted on the election of parish priests by the people and the liquidisation of Church property so that it could be given to the poor. Others wanted an end to the pope's temporal powers, seeing this as the first step in a larger spiritual regeneration.[1]

All these writers distanced themselves from Catholic circles which saw in the crisis of the *ancien régime* the need for a return to medieval Christianity, a civil consortium controlled by the hierarchy. Likewise, they disagreed with Catholics who merely sought a restoration of the alliance between throne and altar. They saw the laicisation of the State and in particular the introduction of religious liberty as an occasion for ridding the Church of accretions gathered over a thousand year long involvement in political power. At the same time they restated their view that only religion could be an adequate basis and legitimation of social life. Within the secular city—where proclamation of the values of liberty and equality allowed citizens to differ more in their views and thereby be less united—the Church remained the only force capable of promoting those social virtues making it possible to live together in an ordered society.

Thus the expression 'Christian Democracy' harboured a substantial ambiguity from its outset: acceptance of the modern world and its values did not lead to the point of abandoning the Church's fundamental guiding role in society. Some writers, e.g. the Franciscan R. Bartoli (1747–1806) did advance the view that Christianity, enabled by the Revolution to return to its evangelical purity, was not only a focus for the consolidation of revolutionary ideas, but also a criterion for judging them and overcoming any injustices inherent in them. However these ideas were only broached and not fully worked out. In general there was the conviction that democracy had to be Christian or it could not survive; the Church, even though stripped of its traditional political privileges, would still—by hegemony rather than coercion—act as the irreplaceable guide in defining the values of society and State.

However, during the course of the nineteenth century the expression seems to have been forgotten. This period saw the growth in strength and confidence of the bourgeois classes, particularly after the creation of the single State in 1861. The Church, for its part, was trying to make up for its loss of support from the secular arm and the end of its temporal power by the promotion of a Catholic movement of laity—mainly in country districts and led by the aristocracy. Here the main project was the reconstruction of medieval Christianity. Believers who were more open towards the modern world regrouped themselves under the name of liberal Catholicism. Towards the end of the century the term was taken up by a group of young people actively involved in social work within the Congress. To this organisation Rome had entrusted the task of ensuring a Catholic presence within liberal Italy while maintaining the intransigent line on the keeping open of the question of temporal power. Of course they did not align themselves with revolutionary experience, but they saw the problems posed by the country's industrialisation, the expansion of the Socialist movement and their first confrontation with mass society as a challenge requiring a redefinition of the relationship between Church and world. In their view 'Christian Democracy' summed up what was needed.

2. FROM MURRI TO STURZO

Beyond local initiatives—such as the publication of periodicals *Christian*

Democracy in Turin, edited by G. Piovano and *The Christian Democratic Union* in Naples edited by G. Avolio, and F. Invrea's proposal to hold a festival of Christian Democracy every year on 15 May—there was also the Pisan Professor G. Toniolo's (1845–1918) plan to produce, in the wake of *Rerum Novarum* and contemporary experience of the European Catholic movement, an initial doctrinal re-systematisation of the idea of Christian democracy. In opposition to the Jesuit G. Chiaudano, who in a short work had severely criticised the use of the term, Toniolo published a paper in 1897 in the *Rivista internazionale di scienze sociali* with the significant title: 'The Concept of Christian Democracy'. In this he ruled out the idea that Christian Democracy had an immediate bearing on politics, or 'upset the natural and historical hierarchy of classes', or implied a change in the laws of property. Rather, Christian democracy was 'that civil order in which all social, juridical and economic forces in the fullness of their hierarchical development co-operate in due measure to the common good, ultimately resulting in the benefit of the lower classes'.[2] As a consequence of this objective it was necessary for the Church to repeat the task it had done in the middle ages: take up the reins, through the papacy, of the process of social development.

In this way the term gained new respectability. A group of young people gathered round the review *Cultura sociale politica e letteraria* edited by the Marchigian priest R. Murri (1870–1944) began putting Toniolo's ideas into practice. They were agreed on the need to push the Congress from the position it occupied—intransigent opposition to the liberal State (*non expedit* to Catholics taking part in elections) and practical social conservatism—and to involve Catholics in the Italian State with a plan for democratic change: adoption of the system of proportional representation and universal suffrage, the practice of holding referendums, widespread administrative centralisation. Differences quickly developed within the group.

Murri, although regarding the Church as the ultimate guarantor of the social order, questioned certain cardinal points of social doctrine. In his opinion, Christian democracy not only implied free organisation of trade unions in the working classes—rejecting the traditional idea of mixed corporations—it also implied full acceptance of modern freedoms and the Church's renunciation of its traditional claim to liberty as its privilege. On the other hand another member of the same group F. Meda (1869–1939) held that democratic institutions were merely the best means of fostering the growth of a Catholic party which would have total control over the civil life of the nation. This would have led to the reconstruction of a Christian regime, whereas Murri questioned the ideological grounds which had led the Church to contemplate with satisfaction the return to medieval Christian society, i.e. the idea that present ills derived from refusal to recognise the Church's authority over human affairs, which had begun with the Protestant Reformation and led on to the long genealogy of modern errors: the French Revolution, liberalism, Socialism, Communism. Instead of cultivating this mythical reconstruction of history, Murri thought Catholics ought really to confront the modern world and in that light to criticise those aspects of Christian culture which had driven the Church to separate itself further and further from human progress.[3] Thus he thought Christian democracy still had a task of religious renewal (not without internal contradictions while Catholicism was still regarded as the ultimate regulator of social relationships), which challenged certain tenets of the current model of Christianity.

These tendencies and especially the growing differences within the Congress—where the Christian democrat young people had decided to develop their movement independently of the Congress—led Leo XIII to intervene. On 18 January 1901 he published the encyclical *Graves de communi*, in which he defined the orthodox view of Christian democracy. On the one hand, the pope legitimated the use of the term but, on the other, he narrowly limited its scope, specifying that it should 'drop any political meaning and signify only beneficent Christian action for the sake of the people'. In an attempt to maintain the unity of the Catholic movement Leo XIII then stressed that the work of believers in social action should be subordinate to the leadership of the hierarchy. Thus he ruled out forms which might be dangerous to the established order. The authoritative Jesuit review *Civiltà cattolica*, which had always been cautious about Christian democratic tendencies, finally clarified the meaning of papal intervention. Recognition of the autonomy of the working classes in their claim to political and civil rights to improve their lot ceased to be a matter of opinion from the moment when the pope had denied its religious orthodoxy. Even if Toniolo and Meda could accept this imposition, Murri could not. In a work written during the second half of 1901 he defined Christian democracy as 'direct participation of the people (...) with particular reference to the poorest and most numerous classes, in economic and political institutions'. From this followed the need for direct intervention by the workers in the conduct of political affairs and control of the means of production.

At first he tried to give an interpretation of the encyclical favourable to his position. But when the Sacred Congregation for Extraordinary Ecclesiastical Affairs issued the instruction *Nessuno ignora* (27 January 1902), ordering Christian democrats to subordinate themselves without delay to Congress, he realised that there was no room left at all for his views. From then on Murri stressed—without ever completely detaching politics from Christian ethics— the autonomy of the politico-social task from the religious sphere, stressing in particular the need to free the personal politics of Catholics from the control of the hierarchy.[4] The death of Leo XIII and the election of Pius X to the papacy, who was quite close to the old intransigent line of the Congress but was also convinced of the opportunity to soften the *non expedit*, in order to oppose the advance of Socialism, brought about a change. In 1904 the Congress was dissolved and Catholics were permitted to take part—to some extent—in the elections, as a force in fact subordinate to the liberals for a united defence of the political, economic and social status quo. The following year saw the emergence of a new unifying organism, the Popular Catholic Union. Its programme was drawn up by Toniolo and ruled out the ferments of Murri's Christian democracy. In fact it laid down that the laity should leave 'custody of the highest informing and guiding principles to the clergy in their authoritative hierarchy' and concern themselves with 'vindicating the Christian social order (...) and translating it in practice into the institutions and life of the nation.'[5]

Although some of the young submitted, Murri decided to form a new autonomous group, the National Democratic League (November 1905). Although it made interesting practical proposals, this organisation had a stunted life which foundered on a fundamental contradiction: the claim to autonomy and independence of politics from Catholicism did not prevent their proclamation of total submission to the Church in the sphere of religious action.[6] The encyclical *Pieni l'animo* of 1906 forbade priests to join the League. The following year Murri—now supporting social modernism—was suspended *a divinis* and in 1909 excommunicated. These measures and the reaction of the Marchigian priest—who tried to transform the League into a sort of mini-church bearing the truth against Rome's 'betrayal'—led to the end of the Christian democrat experience. However a tiny group continued to pursue the initial themes of the movement, even though this was often limited to proclaiming, as did G. Donati (1880–1931) in a famous speech in 1915 'that it is possible to be wholly Catholic without being anti-democratic and seriously democratic without being anti-Catholic.'[7]

After the First World War a number of the people involved reappeared in a movement launched by a Sicilian Priest L. Sturzo (1871–1959). This had formed from the trade union activities promoted by Murrian Christian democracy and then withdrawn into purely local action when it got into trouble with the hierarchy. In 1919 Don Sturzo founded the Italian Popular Party, which arose as 'a non-catholic, non-denominational party, a party with a strong democratic content and inspired by Christian ideals but not taking religion as an element of political difference'. This was also the end of Catholic political unity, when the Holy See made clear its reservations towards a movement which had again stepped outside the Christian perspective.[8] In effect the hierarchy, after having encouraged the constitution of a right wing to determine the party's activity, abandoned it in favour of a direct agreement with Fascism in order to obtain the advantages and privileges it had been seeking for some while. In this framework sanctioned by the Lateran Pacts (1929), in which totalitarian Church and State ruled side by side, only a few people continued to propound Christian democrat ideas from exile.[9]

3. CHRISTIAN DEMOCRACY AFTER THE SECOND WORLD WAR

Between summer and autumn 1942 two groups were formed—one round A. de Gasperi (1881–1954) in Rome and the other round P. Malvestiti (1899–1964) in Milan. They began to tackle the problems of the presence of Catholics in the Italian state in anticipation of the fall of the Fascist regime, now regarded as inevitable. In October of the same year the name Christian Democracy was chosen for these groups, in order to stress their difference from the popular party. In July 1943 De Gasperi published a short work called *Idee riconstruttive della democrazia cristiana*, in which various writers collaborated. This defined the programme of the new political organism: the democratic platform—pluralism, decentralisation, representation—went with a sprinkling of social reform. The relationship with the Church is defined fairly clearly. Through being non-denominational it sought the political unity of Catholics, so as to involve the hierarchy. The Church is seen as the inspirer of moral values in social life and the great carrier of popular consent to democracy.[10]

The attitude of the Holy See, which in the final years of the war was quite amenable—although it did not give up in advance relations with other emerging Catholic political movements, whether of the right or left[11]—tended to favour Christian Democracy. A number of common values and positions emerged: firstly, the thesis that only the Church is the bearer of a valid project of renewal for the whole of society. Secondly, the view that only Catholics, because they are devoted children of the Church, have the moral qualities necessary to run the State rightly. The papacy and the Christian democratic leaders agreed that the construction of a proper democracy needed a sort of ecclesiastical guarantee; on the one hand, ample room is given to the *magisterium* to influence political and civil life and, on the other, Catholics are propounded as exclusively fit to govern the country. This ideological agreement found its counterpart on the organisational plane. At this time Christian democracy lacked its own apparatus and therefore it made use of the structures, and also of the personnel of Catholic Action. In the view of Pius XI Catholic Action was to be a sort of reservoir of personnel obedient to the hierarchy's orders and ready to occupy the principal social positions in the construction of a 'Christian State'. Undoubtedly between '45 and '47 differences emerged in the political views of the hierarchy and of Christian democracy. The former tended to want head-on confrontation with the left-wing parties, whereas the Christian democrats more prudently and with a view to the international scene, looked for collaboration. But the two views, instead of being alternatives seemed to complement each other in the attainment of a Catholic hegemony, which was in fact ratified by the elections of 18 April 1948. This was due to the mobilisation of 'civic committees', a parallel organisation to Catholic Action—whose members it used. They were able to add a large number of moderates and conservatives to the Christian democrat poll.

However there was a group within Christian democracy—gathered round G. Dossetti and the review *Cronache sociali*—which were anxious to keep a clear Maritain-like distinction between spiritual action and more properly political action.[12] Their efforts at cultural renewal and the promotion of a Catholic laity was blocked by their desire to remain in complete submission to the hierarchy, whom they nevertheless regarded as too involved in worldly matters. This group shortly met with resounding political defeat. In fact after the Atlantic choice of the Italian government and the elections of 1948, which marked the end of the tripartite alliance of Christian democracy with the Socialist and Communist parties, the Dossettians, now from a centrist position, pressed for a reformism nurtured on the agreement of the great popular forces present in the country. De Gasperi's reply—probably encouraged by the hierarchy—was fairly hard: the group was accused of trying to open itself up to the Communists and of putting Catholic political unity in jeopardy. By 1951 the tendency dissolved and Dossetti began on a personal course which led to the priesthood and then to a monastery. This seems fairly indicative of the Italian situation: the hierarchy's desire to intervene in political and civil affairs meant the abandonment of proposed reforms. And we should not forget that De Gasperi's line—beyond his own personal moderate views and Christian perspective—leads back to a complex ancestry, in which the authoritative *Civiltà cattolica* and conservative trends in the curia threatened to create a Catholic party, which would be rigidly denominational and politically towards the right.[13] The attempt to involve old Don Sturzo in an approach by the Rome administration to the monarchists and neofascists (1952) marked this tendency's culmination and also its defeat.

Thus the party chose a 'centrist' line, which beyond political contingencies—such as the defeat of the attempt to attribute a majority to Christian democracy (1953)—implied a continual effort to mediate interests expressed by civil society but without ever touching areas of privilege or centres of power.

Here we have the main characteristics of Italian Christian democracy: failure of the initial project for wholesale renewal of society—which anchorage to the Church was to have guaranteed but which the Church leadership proved incapable of delivering—degenerated into a seizure of all the levers of power to safeguard (through a close network of client relations) personal or ecclesiastical interests.[14]

A. Fanfani's succession to De Gasperi (1954) brought a strengthening of organisation, greater independence from the Church apparatus, reduction in links with private industry following the creation of State industry. It was also a generational change but without any effect on the political line and above all without any cultural deepening of what was meant by the party's 'Christian inspiration', although this was constantly referred to.[15]

Undoubtedly there were people in the Italian Catholic world who were strongly critical of this situation, such as Don P. Mazzolari (1890–1959) who in the periodical *Adesso*, censored by the Church authorities, insisted on the need for Christian revolution. We may also recall Don Milani's three proposals when faith was lost in Christian democracy's ability to bring about the country's real social and religious renewal: return to the *non expedit* to avoid any involvement in civil power; actual attainment of the justice preached in the Church's social doctrine; clear distinction between the functions of clergy and laity, prophetic denunciation being a task reserved to the former. The various possibilities implicit in this position show how the Christian perspective still persisted. They also show the growth of criticism of the Church's relationship, through Christian democracy, with civil society.[16]

The papacy of John XXIII, with his simple style of service, his distinction between movements and ideologies, his appeal to all people of good will, his self-distancing from centres of power, seemed to signal a change to which the Second Vatican Council responded only in part. In its documents, especially those on the relationship between the Church and the world, the line of mere Christian 'witness' is juxtaposed with that of Christian social 'presence' in order to play a more effective part in areas of power. In this complex context Christian democracy managed to form an alliance with the Socialists—taking a centre-left line, which was at first condemned by the *Osservatore Romano*, *Civilitá cattolica* and even a declaration by the Holy Office. This option was supported by the party's claim to autonomy described by A. Moro (1916–1978) in the 1962 congress as 'responsibility and risk' of 'bearing witness to Christian values in social life'. But the party's slowness to accept the spirit of Vatican II induced certain fringes of the Catholic world traditionally linked with Christian democracy to detach themselves from it.[17] These happenings, marked by the Holy See by a cautious but firm drive towards

Church renewal, made it necessary to stress the need for Catholic political unity. The two referendums—on divorce in 1974 and abortion in 1981 in Italy—resulted in the defeat of the Christian democrat position but strengthened the links between hierarchy and party. After the death of Paul VI (1978), who, while insisting on the need for a Christian-inspired party had attempted to guarantee it a certain autonomy, the pressures to return to a preconciliar model became stronger. On the other hand, the tendency has emerged to question the central issue: instead of being a help, is a Christian party not an obstacle to the preaching of the Gospel to the democratic secular city?

Translated by Dinah Livingstone

Notes

1. V. E. Giuntella 'Il cattolicesimo democratico nel triennio giacobino' *Cattolicesimo e lumi nel Settecento italiano* ed. M. Rosa (Rome 1981) pp. 267–294.
2. G. Toniolo *Democrazia cristiana. Concetti e indirizzi*, I (Città del Vaticano 1949) p. 26.
3. G. Are *I cattolici e la questione sociale in Italia (1894–1904)* (Milan 1963) pp. 26–58.
4. *Romolo Murri nella storia politica e religiosa del suo tempo* ed. G. Rossini (Rome 1972).
5. G. Toniolo *Iniziative culturali e di azione cattolica* (Città del Vaticano 1951) p. 13.
6. C. Giovannini *Politica e religione nel pensiero della lega Democratica Nazionale* (Rome 1968).
7. G. Donati *Scritti politici* ed. G. Rossini (Rome 1956) p. 249.
8. G. Miccoli 'Chiesa e società in Italia fra '800 e '900' in *Fra mito della cristianità e secolarizzazione* (Casale Monferrato 1985) pp. 82–85.
9. G. Fanello Marcucci *Alle origini della democraziz cristiana (1929–44)* (Brescia 1982).
10. P. Scoppola *La proposta politica di De Gasperi* (Bologna 1977).
11. G. Ruggieri and R. Albani *Cattolici comunisti? Originalità e contraddizioni di una esperienza lontana* (Brescia 1978).
12. G. Miccoli 'Chiesa, partito cattolico e società civile (1945–1975)' in the work cited in note 8 at pp. 397–409.
13. A. Riccardi *Il 'partito romano' nel secondo dopoguerra (1945–1954)* (Brescia 1983).
14. G. Baget-Bozzo *Il partito cristiano al potere* (Florence 1974).
15. P. Scoppola 'Democrazia cristiana' in *Dizionario storico del movimento cattolico in Italia* ed. F. Traniello and G. Campanini, 1/2 (Casale Monferrato 1981) pp. 257–277.

16. G. Miccoli 'Don Lorenzo Milani nella chiesa del suo tempo' in the work cited in note 8 at pp. 428–54.

17. G. Martina *La chiesa in Italia negli ultimi trent'anni* (Rome 1977).

René Rémond

The Case of France

IN THE European range of political expressions of Christian Democracy
France is a singular case. Its originality is due to three main features. First, it
has the longest history, almost 200 years if the distant origins of the
phenomenon are traced back to the unsuccessful attempts to reconcile loyalty
to the Church with the principles of democracy at the time of the French
revolution. It is appropriate that the forerunners of Christian democracy
should have appeared in France since it was also in France that, for the first
time in Europe, a people began to proclaim the values of democracy.
Nonetheless Christian Democracy did not establish itself in France as a
durable force, in contrast to most of the other countries concerned, where the
history of Christian Democracy was one of continuous growth to the point at
which it became (in several countries) the main political force. The history of
Christian Democracy in France is broken, jerky, made up of sudden
appearances followed by long eclipses. This is its second characteristic. In this
it reflects a characteristic feature of French political history, divided as it is by
revolutionary breaks.

For a quarter of a century now the movement which drew its inspiration
from Christian democracy has been more or less absent from the political
scene. This is the third characteristic feature of the French case. For reasons
which it is important to elucidate and to which I shall return, France has never
known a real denominational party. The approximations to Christian
Democracy which it has practised at certain moments of its political history
have always taken care to avoid establishing a direct link between religion and
politics.

72

1. THREE PRECURSORY EPISODES OF CHRISTIAN DEMOCRACY

The first of these occasions, which reveals the outline of a future Christian Democracy, was a failure the consequences of which cast a lasting shadow over its future. This is the history of the Constitutional Church between 1790 and 1794. One name personifies the best of this venture, that of Abbé Grégoire, a figure who typifies those priests who believed for a time that it was possible to reconcile their fidelity to the priesthood with loyalty to the new institutions adopted by France. The experiment was doomed to failure. In unilaterally overturning the internal organisation of the Church, the members of the Constituent Assembly, who had no concept of the modern idea of secularity in the form of the juridical expression of the distinction between the domain of individual conscience and what falls under the authority of the State, brought down on themselves the condemnation of the Holy See. The Vatican found it all the harder to deal with this interference in that, unlike the regalian interventions of princes, it invoked principles which at the time seemed to the Church contrary to the Christian definition of a person's duties to God and society. As a result, this experiment in Christian Democracy paid the price of the ideological and political confrontation between the revolution and Catholicism. The episode was long to burden its future; in the eyes of the majority of Catholics the very idea of democracy remained identified with militant hostility to religion, and its applications seemed incompatible with loyalty to the faith.

The second episode was equally short-lived, nor did it have a happier ending: it is linked to the name of La Mennais and the revolution of July 1830. In truth, its origins were not democratic at all. La Mennais' abandonment of reaction, of which he had been one of the most renowned theorists and advocates was due primarily to his disappointment at not obtaining the support of the restored monarchy for the revival of a sort of theocracy. He never forgave the Restoration government for not going the whole way and restoring a traditional society and order in which religion would have guided collective behaviour. In reaction he rallied to the popular government, which he hoped would be more open to religious imperatives. Arguing from the revolution which had just overthrown the Bourbons, and faithfully following his philosophy of common sense, which made universal assent the criterion of truth, he concluded that from the downfall of principles and régimes two forces alone emerged intact: God and liberty. They had to be reconciled, and this was the inspiration of the newspaper he edited for several months in 1830–31, *L'Avenir*, which bore that very motto: 'God and liberty'. Ambiguous in its origins, the venture was also premature. Rome remained attached to negotiations with sovereigns, and continued to see the recognition of liberties as a fatal error. The encyclical *Mirari vos* of 1832 marked a break between the Church and the principles of liberty, and *a fortiori* democracy.

The third episode was just as brief and similarly unfruitful. Like the first two, it was connected with a revolution, that of 1848. It began with an idyll between democracy and Christianity: unlike the two previous revolutions, whose inspiration had included feelings of hostility to the Church, that of 1848 invoked the Gospel. A few clerics and a newspaper translated and expressed the great hope of reconciling Church and democracy: Lacordaire, the restorer of the Dominican order, Abbé Maret, future dean of the theology faculty of the Sorbonne, Frédéric Ozanam, founder of the Conferences of St Vincent de Paul and the newspaper *Ère nouvelle*, the title of which, like that of *L'Avenir*, testified to the desire of these Catholics to shift their thinking from nostalgia for the past and turn their eyes towards the future which was to be built. The experiment lasted no more than a few months. Its failure was due this time, less to the Republic's religious policy than to the drift of political events and the history of the Roman question. Pius IX took the events which drove him from Rome as proof of the harmfulness of democratic principles, and found in them yet another argument to confirm his intransigence. Fifteen years later, in 1864, the *Syllabus*, by including among the errors condemned the idea that the Roman Pontiff should come to terms with the principles of modern society, fixed an unbridgeable and apparently permanent gulf between Christianity and democracy. In fact, there were no further ventures of this sort for another 40 years. Between 1850 and 1890 those Catholics who were concerned to give the development of society a Christian orientation were inspired by a reactionary ideology and offered, as the sole legitimate transcription of Christian revelation for political societies, a social philosophy which was conservative, hierarchical, inegalitarian and authoritarian.

2. RALLYING TO THE REPUBLIC

Christian Democracy enjoyed its first spring in the years 1890–1910, in the wake of the urgent invitation addressed by Pope Leo XIII to Catholics to rally to the Republic. This move was not in the beginning a conversion to democracy; it was no more than acceptance of the regime. Since the institutions and the republican form of the State manifestly enjoyed the support of the majority of the people, it would have been impolitic for the Church to remain linked to parties which nourished the dream of an improbable restoration. The issue was the preservation of religious interests, not acceptance of democracy. However, by freeing the Church from an association—which sometimes went as far as identification—with the enemies of democracy, Rome's initiative opened the way to Christian democracy, just as in 1926 the condemnation by Pius XI of Action Française was to encourage the emergence of a different form of Christian democracy. These examples show how far the fate of Christian democracy in France was dependent, for good—as in 1890 and 1926—or ill—as in 1791, 1832 and 1849—on interventions from Rome. In the wake of this political shift a generation of young priests threw themselves headlong into social action, journalism and politics. These were the 'democratic priests' (*abbés démocratiques*), who won much sympathy among the younger clergy. One of the most representative and most respected figures was Abbé Lemire, a priest from the north, who was deputy for Hazebrouck from 1893 until his death in 1928. Alongside, from 1894, arose a movement whose nature is not easy to define, partly youth movement, partly learned society, *Le Sillon*, whose driving force was a man who was to leave his mark on a whole generation, and whose name even today is a symbol: Marc Sangnier, inspiring leader, incomparable orator, generous visionary. *Le Sillon* took up its position deliberately and unreservedly on the democratic side: its ambition was to reconcile once and for all Church and people, Christianity and democracy. Its creed was that democracy, far from being alien to the Gospel, was its political equivalent. Was it not the teaching of Jesus which taught people that they were equal in dignity and rights? Conversely, democracy needs Christianity to overcome the obstacles of individual egoism. This first golden age of Christian democracy was criss-crossed with setbacks which dimmed its brightness, such as the crisis of the Dreyfus affair. It encountered fierce resistances and, from 1900 onwards, came into conflict with increasing incomprehension on the part of Rome, culminating in 1910 with the condemnation of *Le Sillon*, which was suspect for having linked Catholicism and democracy too closely. It was the revenge of those Catholics who were the implacable enemies of democratic ideas. This time their victory was to be shorter-lived than before.

The 1914–18 war hastened the reconciliation between the Church and the Republic, and the ending of the religious quarrel made *rapprochements* possible. This second movement towards democracy created the conditions for a rebirth of a Christian-inspired democracy. The qualification, 'Christian-inspired', is important. Henceforth the pioneers took care to avoid over-explicit reference to religion. This was not because of any shame at admitting their convictions, nor a tactical ploy: the Catholics who intended to work for the reconciliation of the Church and democracy did so in the name of pluralism and the freedom of Christians to choose their political convictions. They based their position on the distinction of planes, the temporal and the spiritual; they did not challenge the right of others who shared their faith to hold different opinions, but claimed that right for themselves. This form of

Christian Democracy drew its sources of inspiration and its troops equally from social Catholicism (where an open and forward-looking version had largely replaced the traditionalist outlook), from Christian trade unionism (since 1919 the various unions, the oldest dating back to 1886, had been regrouping in the French Confederation of Christian Workers (CFTC), and from the men who had undergone their civic apprenticeship in the Association Catholique de la Jeunesse Française founded by Albert de Mun in 1886, which had developed from its traditionalist positions towards a democratic outlook.

In 1924 those who shared this outlook created for the first time a political instrument in the form of the Parti Démocratique Populaire ('Popular Democratic Party')—note that the title deliberately made no explicit reference to the Church—which organised like the classical political parties, put up candidates at elections and had about 15 deputies in the parliaments of 1928, 1932 and 1936. This party had dedicated activists and enjoyed the support of a few daily newspapers, notably *L'Aube*, edited by Francisque Gay, who sought to make it the focus of all the tiny Christian-inspired democratic groups, and a regional daily, *Ouest-Eclair*, in Rennes. But the party remained too weak in parliament to have much influence and suffered from its position between a conservative right which retained the confidence of most Catholics and a left which continued to see the Church as a force for conservatism. In 1936, forced to take sides, it went right, while the *Jeune République*, another heir to the tradition of Marc Sangnier, joined the Popular Front.

3. THE MOUVEMENT RÉPUBLICAIN POPULAIRE (MRP)

For the Christian-inspired democratic movement the successive trials of the war and the defeat, the German occupation, the underground struggle against the enemy and opposition to the Vichy regime were the occasion of a mutation and above all of spectacular growth. In the underground struggle the Christian Democrats, better informed than their fellow citizens about the nature of National Socialism, were among the first to reject any accomodation with the enemy. They became aware of their attachment to democratic values, and saw the need to widen the base of their organisation, laying the foundations of a movement which they envisaged as bringing together all those who wanted to base democracy on humanist principles. This was the MRP, founded officially a few weeks after the Liberation, in November 1944. The first elections, in spring 1945, revealed that the party's programme had wide public support. A few months later, at the elections for the Constituent Assembly, the MRP emerged as an important political force: it received a quarter of the votes, its parliamentary group numbered 160 deputies, and it shared power with the Socialist and Communist parties under the authority of General de Gaulle. At one point it was even to be the largest party in France. Thereafter the MRP was hardly ever out of government until the fall of the Fourth Republic in 1958: thus for 12 years the Christian Democrats were to have the opportunity to influence public policy.

How and why did the small pre-1940 party become the great post-1945 movement? At the time the MRP was the only relatively new movement which had had no responsibility for the mistakes of the pre-war period: it met the aspiration for a renewal of political life. Moreover, it presented itself as a movement which wanted to invent a type of political behaviour different from that of the classical political parties. It also undoubtedly benefited from the feeling that it was the group closest to General de Gaulle; in the absence at the time of any Gaullist group admiration for the leader of the resistance acted in its favour. It also benefited from the disappearance of the right-wing parties and from the discredit into which their ideas had fallen as France emerged from the occupation. The electorate pulled it to the right, the activists pulled it to the left. This strain partly explains its fate and prefigures its failure. Most important, it gathered the fruits of 15 years of solid work by Christian activists. The new party combined the legacy of social Catholicism, the experience of Christian trade unionists, the dynamism of the specialised movements of the Association Catholique de la Jeunesse Française (JOC, JEC, JAC), whose militants had served their apprenticeship for responsibility in the resistance. In the MRP the complete integration of Catholics into political society was achieved: the commitment to democracy shown in the resistance and the proof of their sincere and genuine acceptance of the Republic meant that their republicanism could no longer be questioned. The MRP shared many positions with the Socialists, and at one moment a wide labour grouping was being considered, to include both Christians and secularists. Though the idea came to nothing, the religious issue was nonetheless dead. Initially the MRP took up a position much further left than the PDP: the whole system of political forces had moved left. As a result, the MRP was responsible for the political education of a mass of Catholics, whom it brought to socially more advanced positions than their traditional outlooks.

The MRP was a novelty not only in the French political system, but also in comparison with the European Christian Democrat parties. We have already noted that its title contained no reference to Christianity, and the same was true of its constitution and programme. This reveals a peculiar and essential feature of the French case. Despite the tendency, frequent both in France and abroad, to identify the MRP and Christian democracy, the MRP was not a denominational party. The absence of any denominational reference was neither hypocrisy nor prudence dictated by electoral tactics. It was intended as the expression of a fact and of a hope. While the party enjoyed privileged relations with the Church and its membership was made up in the great majority of Catholics brought to politics by spiritual conviction, it was open to people of any religion. It never enjoyed the public support of the religious authorities: in contrast to the practice in some countries, the French bishops never made it an obligation in conscience for Catholics to vote only for MRP candidates. Moreover, except perhaps in 1945–46, when there was as yet no right-wing group to attract their votes,the MRP never received a majority of Catholic votes; they were divided between the MRP, the conservative and liberal right represented by the Independents, and the opposition Gaullism represented from 1947 by the RPF (*Rassemblement du Peuple Français*). This dispersion of Catholic sympathies is a constant of French political history. In every period and under every regime French Catholics, long before it was recognised as legitimate by the Church, have practised pluralism of political choices, probably because they always resisted confusion between the religious and the political, and because even those with the greatest respect for religious authority always rejected clericalism. In France concern for the State's independence of the Church and attachment to individual freedom in politics are phenomena as old as the practice of universal suffrage and the emergence of political democracy.

On the other hand, for all the MRP's caution about denominational involvements, its very existence was regarded by some Christians, intellectuals and activists, as still too heavily marked by denominational links. Emmanuel Mounier and the journal *Esprit*, who were hostile in principle to any compromise of religious values with governmental expediency, maintained a severe and sometimes unjust criticism of the MRP and its policies. Many activists, too, mainly workers but also students and teachers, criticised the MRP for encouraging confusion and attacked the very notion of Christian democracy.

Over the years the gulf between the MRP and a section of French Catholicism was to widen ever further. The breakdown of the agreement with the left-wing parties and the enforced ties with liberal and conservative groups brought about a drift to the right by the MRP which first disappointed and later revolted a section of its activists. The exercise of responsibilities forced its leaders to follow, especially in the colonies, a policy which clashed with the generous aspirations of the Catholic left. Above all, its stubborn opposition to Pierre Mendès-France, who enjoyed the sympathies of the new generation of Catholic activists, finally cut the MRP off from its sources and dried up the sources of fresh leadership. At the end of the Fourth Republic the MRP was rejected on the right, as much through the general evolution of the system of forces as for any action of its own. It was identified with the fallen regime, just as, 20 years earlier, the Radical Party had been identified with the Third Republic, and shared this fate with the Socialist Party. After 1960 the generation which became active in politics defined itself by rejecting the old parties: the MRP was the target of young Catholics, the SFIO of its followers, and the Communist Party was to be overtaken on the left by the rebirth of an extreme left. In other words, the phenomenon was general, and in the case of the MRP it was combined with criticism of the very principle that membership of the Church and adherence to its teachings should or could be manifested in a political grouping.

From 1962 the MRP went into hibernation. Its leaders put it into suspended animation and worked for the birth of a broader movement, an initiative which received a response only on the right, among the Independents. The men and women who had passed through the MRP scattered in all directions, from the extreme right to the Socialist left. Georges Bidault, one of the most eminent personalities of the MRP, having been its president as well as a former leader-writer on the pre-war L'Aube, successor to Jean Moulin as head of the National Council of the Resistance, president of the provisional government after the withdrawal of General de Gaulle, and foreign minister and prime minister under the Fourth Republic, became an implacable opponent of General de Gaulle, even supporting the OAS and attempts to remove de Gaulle by violence. Other equally prominent figures went over to the Gaullist parties and accepted ministerial responsibilities in the governments of the Fifth Republic: an example is Maurice Schumann, the MRP's first president. Its last president, Jean Lacanuet, stood in the 1965 presidential election against de Gaulle, and forced him into a second round of voting. Others became supporters of Mendès-France, and others again joined the Socialist movement after 1970 and took part in the renewal of the Socialist Party. The MRP began to look like a way-station, and its descendants became a diaspora.

4. THE SITUATION TODAY

What is left of it today? For the record we may note a small grouping which revived the title 'Christian Democrat', following a former MRP leader, Alfred Coste-Floret, and with the support of some friends of the industrialist Marcel Dassault; it differs little in its programme from the most conservative section of the right. The CDS (Centre des démocrates sociaux) or Social Democratic Centre, which is a full member of the right-wing majority and has several members in Jacques Chirac's government, is beyond doubt the most legitimate heir of the old MRP and the last trace of French Christian democracy. This group includes many people who began their political activity in the MRP. In addition, there are various signs that, after seeming to forget its origins for some years, the CDS today is anxious to go back to its roots and to affirm its identity in terms of the democratic Catholic tradition. Could this be the sign of a revival of the idea in France?

This brief survey of an eventful history, made up of distinct sections, eclipses and resurgences, has shown that the French experience is unique. France has not had a denominational party analogous to those which have played an important role in the political history of Germany, Italy, Belgium, the Netherlands, Austria and a number of other countries. This uniqueness is puzzling. Some partial explanations may be suggested. In Germany and the Netherlands the formation of a denominational party was a means whereby a religious minority could preserve its identity and win equal rights. France was almost wholly Catholic, but so was Italy, which yet has a Christian Democrat party.

The real explanation is probably to be found in the French cultural tradition which has always had its own view of the relationship between politics and religion: on the one hand, an instinctive repugnance for 'government by *curés*', an old anti-clerical instinct, on the other, an elevated view of religious belief which will not tolerate its degradation in the contingencies of political choices. The conjunction of these opposing attitudes has prevented the formation of denominational parties and blocked the emergence of Christian democracy. In this respect, as perhaps in others, France is not like its neighbours.

Translated by Francis McDonagh

Michael Fleet

Case Study: Chile

SINCE 1982 the dictatorship of Chilean General Augusto Pinochet has been rocked by economic and political crises. Its once substantial support has fallen sharply, and opposition to it, although still not unified, has broadened and intensified. In this context, and despite more than a decade of virtual inactivity, the Christian Democratic party (PDC) is exhibiting renewed vigour and promise. Its militants are leading figures in revived student, labour, and popular social movements. It has retained most of its traditional electoral following. And having opposed both the Popular Unity (1970–73) and military governments, it is a leading candidate to head a post-military government if and when transition comes.

The Christian Democrats are not without their problems, however. They have never been able to work with the Chilean left, and are still not 'trusted' by either the right or left, each of which continues to suspect them of seeking to absorb its following. During the years of military rule, moreover, they have been challenged and occasionally outflanked by more radical Christians linked to organisations and projects sponsored by the Chilean Catholic Church. And finally, as in the past, the Christian Democrats remain internally divided on basic questions of objectives, strategy, and alliance partners.

In this context, the party's future prospects are unclear. It may lead the transition, if indeed one takes place, but will find it difficult to govern without alienating one of its internal factions. An exodus of significant numbers of either could produce important political realignments, and could give rise to a sizeable left-wing Christian party or movement. But it is also possible that few would leave, and that radical Christians will be drawn instead to one of the secular left parties. An informed assessment of the prospects of Chilean

Christian Democracy at this juncture requires that we look at its historical experience and at the political context within which it has operated.

1. CHRISTIAN DEMOCRACY 1950–86

Emerging initially in the mid-1930s, Chilean Christian Democracy spent several decades in relative obscurity. The 1950s and early 1960s, however, were years of spectacular growth and expansion. Thanks to the rising personal popularity of Eduardo Frei, and to a growing sense that centre and right-wing rivals could no longer keep the Marxist left at bay, the party drew workers, peasants, marginals, and women to its ranks. Within a span of less than ten years, it went from virtual insignificance to become the country's largest single party. When Frei was elected president in 1964 expectations of a new Christian Democratic era in Chilean politics were widespread.

Following two years of economic and political prosperity, however, the Christian Democrats were engulfed by the same demands and tensions that helped bring them to power. In effect, they were unable to allay the fears of a nervous and sceptical right, but in attempting to do so alienated the left and many of their own progressive elements as well. The Frei government could boast of significant accomplishments, but was unable to jar the economy loose from its longstanding log-jam. As a result, the political polarisation it vowed to transcend grew sharper, eroding the party's political base, helping to revive political rivals it had hoped to render obsolete, and leading to widespread unrest and conflict during the last two years of its term.[1]

A major factor in the party's failure was its unwillingness to bargain seriously for either right- or left-wing support. The Christian Democrats had long portrayed themselves as an alternative to politics as conceived and practiced by political rivals. In this spirit Frei sought to carry out his Revolution in Liberty without modifications or concessions, in effect polarising political options and hoping to capture the constituencies of both left- and right-wing parties without negotiating with their leaders. Unfortunately, he failed to win additional converts and succeeded instead in intensifying the will to resist in those sectors—organised labor and the business community—whose cooperation was needed if his social and economic programmes were to succeed.

Ideological division within his own party's ranks compounded Frei's difficulties. The split was between the more pragmatic, but strongly anti-Marxist mainstream (*oficialistas*) and a vigorous democratic Socialist minority (*rebeldes* and *terceristas*). The latter's criticisms of Frei encouraged the Marxist left, and at the same time confirmed right-wing suspicions that the

PDC was at heart a radical political force. *Oficialista* responses, on the other hand, encouraged the right while re-enforcing the left's misgivings. As these forces recovered, the Christian Democrats remained engulfed in dissension and disarray. In May 1969 the better part of their left wing broke away to form the *MAPU*,[2] and in September of the following year, the party's Radomiro Tomic finished behind both victorious Salvador Allende and right-wing runner-up Jorge Alessandri in the presidential election.

This unexpected turn of events confronted the party with a difficult choice. The similarity in Christian Democratic and Popular Unity programmes was a potential basis for collaboration between the two, but the anti-left animus of many leaders and activists had been heightened during the Frei years. Following weeks of acrimonious internal debate, the party decided to support Allende's confirmation by the Congress. Once Allende was seated, however, relations with his government began to deteriorate. Most Christian Democratic leaders anticipated problems, and from early on sought to block his programme and to expand their political base and leverage. More progressive and/or less sceptical elements hoping to support Allende initially prevailed but were quickly lost in the shuffle. The pursuit of partisan political advantage by Marxists and Christian Democrats alike embittered spirits and drove the latter steadily rightwards.

During the second half of 1971 the PDC's 'constructive opposition' gave way to denunciations of 'totalitarian designs' and to frequent confrontations between Christian Democratic and Popular Unity workers, students, civil servants, and peasants. In early 1972, economic and social conditions began to deteriorate badly, as strikes, lockouts, building seizures, protest marches, and mass demonstrations by opposing groups became the regular fare of political life. When the joint Christian Democratic-right wing front won only a modest majority in the March 1973 congressional elections (and thus could not legally force Allende's impeachment), matters reached a final impasse, and rumours of an ultimate reckoning began to circulate. During the final months Christian Democrats encouraged military intervention in both direct and indirect ways, hoping to accede to power themselves, but helping instead to usher in a dictatorship that has ruled the country ever since.

Had the PDC not moved or been pushed to the right, some of Allende's social and economic programmes might have 'worked', and his government might not have collapsed. But with that party joining the right in a united anti-UP front, his fate and the country's were sealed. Internal divisions within each camp, the deepening partisan political antagonism with which each viewed the other, and the fact that neither fully controlled its own elements, all played roles in the deterioration of PDC-UP relations. Allende's efforts to polarise political options were no more productive than Frei's. And his government's lack of clarity regarding basic goals and limits was also a serious problem. In fact, at crucial points throughout the period Christian Democrats and Marxists could agree on specific policy issues but could not overcome their feelings of mutual doubt and mistrust. For some Christian Democrats it did not seem to matter what the UP parties or Allende said or did; trusting them was inconceivable. For others the lack of strong leadership and/or internal consensus within the UP raised doubts as to whether even sincere offers of compromise would be fulfilled.

The period of military rule has been more repressive, more conservative ideologically, and more enduring than anyone initially imagined. The military's ascendancy since the coup has been facilitated by: (a) the intense anxieties and enmities accumulating during the Frei and Allende governments; (b) Pinochet's skilful exploitation of these sentiments in an atmosphere unencumbered by the presence of audible countervailing argument; and (c) the continuing estrangement of Christian Democrats and Marxists.

The party's relations with the military have evolved much as did those with the Allende government. An initial period of limited collaboration was followed by outright though still circumspect opposition (until 1980), and then by active involvement in the oppositionist *Alianza Democratica*. Until recently this group included 'renovated' or democratic Socialists, but pointedly excluded the Communist party, the bulk of the Socialist party, and groups of the Christian left, thereby reflecting the continuing division of anti-military forces.

During the period party factions have been of several minds. Generally speaking, the more progressive, 'social-democratic' *chascon* faction favours a more stridently oppositionist stance, and continues to press for alliance with the left. Rival *quatones*, on the other hand, are more inclined to accept the military's terms for transition, are less interested in reforming (or transforming) existing Capitalist structures, and would prefer to ally with the right.

By the end of the first year there was general consensus that the Junta was a dictatorship with quasi-Fascist leanings, but not on what could or should be done about it. Party leaders did not wish to alienate those supporters who appeared favourably disposed towards the government, and sought to criticise basic economic policy and individual instances of repression without appearing to challenge the military or the process of 'national reconstruction' as such. During the period the Chilean Communist party continued to stress 'peaceful' means of resistance and at various junctures offered to support an anti-Fascist alliance led by the PDC, but the party rejected all suggestions of united centre-left opposition movement.

Following the 1980 plebiscite (that approved a new authoritarian constitution), the party languished in a mixture of depression, indecision, and inactivity. But then came the economic downturn that began in mid-1981, and the surprisingly successful protests of 1983 and 1984, the latter thanks to the efforts of a revived labour movement and Church sponsored neighbourhood and human rights groups. With these developments, the Christian Democrats won a new and unexpected lease on life, and quickly assumed the more resolute oppositionist stance it has maintained since.

The constitution approved in 1980 calls for a plebiscite in 1989, in which voters will be asked to approve or reject a presidential candidate (presumably but not necessarily Pinochet) to be named by the Junta. If the candidate wins majority approval he will serve as president until 1997; if not, Pinochet will remain in power for another year, at the end of which a new president and a congress will be chosen in direct popular elections.

This timetable, together with the dramatic decline in support for the miliary since 1982,[3] makes a return to civilian rule in the relatively near future a distinct possibility. The only trouble, however, is that Pinochet could cancel the plebiscite (fearing he would lose) or use State machinery at his disposal to either win or steal it. A united opposition movement including the traditional left would make the latter alternatives less feasible, and the former more enticing but also more difficult. But unless or until opposition forces come together and begin to project the image of a viable and promising alternative, none of these options can be dismissed or ignored.

In the event of a plebiscite being held, and the military's 'candidate' defeated, the Christian Democrats may well head the post-military government. For one, they appear to have recaptured much of their traditional following.[4] Additionally, they have people and organisational structures in virtually all parts of the country, and their militants are among the most active and influential leaders of revived student, labour, and popular movements. And finally, they hold a middle of the road position at a time when large numbers of Chileans appear disillusioned with 'extremes' of any sort, and both right- and left-wing groups are more favourably disposed toward liberal democratic institutions and moderate reform projects than at any time in recent memory.

But the years since the coup have been difficult ones for the PDC, and it may not be as strong politically or as likely to prevail during the transition or beyond as it might seem at this point.[5] For one, with the death of Eduardo Frei in 1982, the party lost the political figure with whom it rose to national prominence. Further, during the years of military rule, it has lost touch with its electoral following, and has seen former militants drawn into activities and organisations beyond its control and influence.[6] And finally, the party remains divided, as in the past, on questions of basic objectives and strategy, causing left- and right-wing groups to continue to question the party's 'real' intentions and objectives, and thereby inhibiting the formation of a solid opposition front for both the transition and beyond.

During the thirty years since its emergence as a major political force Chilean Christian Democracy has retained its appreciable national following by holding to a strongly anti-Marxist and therefore independent reformist stance. At crucial junctures, however, its fear and distrust of the left has prevented it from forming the alliances needed to carry out reforms or to thwart forces opposing them. The party's internal divisions and strong anti-leftist sentiments are common to most Christian Democratic parties. In the Italian and German cases they have been sources of political strength and appeal, but in Chile, at least to this point, they have hurt both the party and the country as a whole. Whether or not they continue to do so depends on the persistence of certain features and structures of Chilean politics, to which we now turn.

2. THE CONTEXT OF CHILEAN POLITICS

Although of late the object of understandable nostalgia, pre-1973 Chilean politics were hardly ideal even at their best. Formally democratic they nonetheless reflected the highly undemocratic economic, social, and cultural contexts within which they were set. The governments elected between 1936 and 1958 succeeded one another in stable and orderly fashion, but for the most part muddled along failing to address or resolve the country's serious social and economic problems. And when, as under Frei and Allende, attempts at fundamental change were undertaken, its social and political fabric was stretched to and beyond the breaking point.

Two particular features of the political context in which the Chilean Christian Democrats have had to operate are worthy of mention here: the centrality of the State and the executive branch, and the persistence of a fragmented, ideologically distant and highly competitive party system.

From its inception under Spanish colonial rule the Chilean State has exercised direct, extensive, and centralised control over economic resources and both social and economic activities. This fact, coupled with the chronic malaise of the Chilean economy, has made the winning and holding of State power the object of intense ambition and concern by the country's social, economic, and political forces.

Except for the period 1891 to 1925, this strong State has been dominated by a powerful executive branch whose administrative and legislative prerogatives made it the system's principal agency of patronage and decision-making, and the object of fear and desire by all. But even as it grew stronger, the presidency was never entirely free of restraint. The courts and the congress retained certain powers, in the face of which those of the president became a double-edged sword. On the one hand, they could tempt executives to 'go it on their own', and to downgrade the importance of a solid social and political majority in support of their programme. And in the cases of Allende and Frei the failure to pay sufficient attention and/or court to congressional opponents could provoke fatal resistance. And, on the other hand, they kept all parties thinking almost perpetually of their own chances the next time around, and frequently encouraged the premature abandonment of a government by groups initially supportive of it.[7]

A second important aspect of Chilean politics has been the persistence for more than forty years of a tripartite ('three-thirds') division of political forces, in which the left, centre, and right constitute solid blocs with comparable electoral followings.[8] In itself such an alignment need not preclude stable coalitions and/or peaceful coexistence as long as the centre was dominated by forces (the pragmatic *Partido Radical*) willing to align themselves with either the left or the right. But with the ascendancy of the PDC each of the three blocs has tended to define its project in terms that exclude the other two, and coalitions have been virtually impossible.[9]

The persistence of these features would almost certainly be prejudicial to Christian Democrats. On the one hand, a strong presidential State structure makes the party's historic 'alternative project' appear both more plausible to its leadership and more worrisome to its potential allies. And on the other, the rigid three-bloc system makes a potentially costly schism more difficult for the party to avoid. Were the Christian Democrats to abandon their own 'unique' project, and were the other blocs to loosen up, the party could conceivably sustain an alliance with both left- and right-wing partners, and thereby endure and survive its own fragmentation. But if these blocs remain intact, it will have to choose between them, and this will almost certainly provoke an exodus of some proportions.

The terms of the 1980 constitution make the persistence of a strong presidential State a virtual certainty for years to come. The future of the three-block system, however, is less clear. In terms of public support the evidence is mixed. One survey taken early in 1986 reported identical levels (left 34 per cent, centre 33 per cent, and right 33 per cent) for the three, although another, taken in July, discovered greater support for the centre (58 per cent) than for the right (20 per cent) or left (19 per cent).

Regarding the solidity of the blocs, the character of their respective projects, and their attitudes towards one another, trends are even more difficult to define. Both the left and right have undergone renovation and realignment since 1973. Fragmentation has been a problem and tendencies favourable to reformism and to liberal democratic principles and institutions have arisen within each. The once solid right has splintered into three large groups (Nationals, Independent Democrats, and the MUN), and a number of smaller (and more anti-military) tendencies (Liberals and Republicans). On the left, the Communists are divided in terms of strategy, while the Socialists are split into multiple factions and no longer function as a single organisation.

These developments helped bring the PDC and the democratic (Nuñez) faction of the Socialists closer together, and gave rise to a *Democratic Alliance* that included both right- and left-wing groups. Unfortunately, this venture was possible precisely because those involved were marginal to their respective blocs, i.e., they were without organised cadres and/or mass followings, and did not materially affect the Alliance's centrist character.[10] And by the end of 1986 these forces were moving back to their original camps, apparently convinced that they stood a better chance of influencing others from within than from beyond their ranks.

Most right-wing groups remain suspicious of the PDC, and seem to think that the military will relinquish power without being politically pressured or defeated. Left Christians and democratic Socialists, on the other hand, do not believe that a peaceful transition will come, or that there will be stability in subsequent years, until the Communists repudiate armed opposition (a strategy to which they turned following the 1980 plebiscite), and unless their cadres and those of other Socialist factions are welcomed into a united centre-left movement.

Traditional patterns are thus showing renewed strength of late. Alignments and relationships are still too much in flux for one to predict outcomes within or between the various groups, although the persistence of the three-thirds scenario appears to be a distinct possibility. And if it does endure, it is difficult to see how the party can avoid choosing between centre-left and centre-right coalitions and thus alienating a substantial number of militants and supporters.

CONCLUSIONS

Like its counterparts in Europe and Latin America the Chilean Christian Democratic party represents the interests and aspirations of Christians of varying class statuses and ideological persuasions. In relative terms, it has been one of the more progressive, although like others it has been plagued with internal tensions and divisions, and has suffered several important splits over the years. These have hurt it politically at certain junctures, but have not yet been fatal.

The principal division has been between neocapitalist and democratic Socialist wings, although many members and activists would see themselves as fitting somewhere between these poles. The more pragmatic neo-capitalist wing has been the dominant force over the years, although the more progressive wing has played a crucial role at key junctures and appears to enjoy roughly equal footing at this point.

Many moderate or conservative Christian Democrats openly question whether reforms are either politically or economically appropriate at this time. Others remain committed to reform but clearly have reduced their expectations and the risks and/or sacrifices they will endure on its behalf. And yet Christian Democracy continues to generate radical dissenters as well, i.e., militants that have experienced the same disappointments and frustrations, but refuse to give in or settle for less. In many cases they have lived and struggled with industrial workers, the unemployed poor, and the peasantry, and their commitment is less to freedom and human dignity in the abstract than to the people and communities with whose fates they have become largely identified.

That a progressive tendency even survives today is remarkable in view of the defections of 1969 and 1971. In each instance these left the party a more unified and more conservative force, but only temporarily. Defectors were soon replaced by others radicalised by subsequent crises or experiences. Chilean life, it seems, does this periodically to a segment of the socially and politically committed Christian population. The issues, contexts, and organisational expressions change, but the phenomenon persists.

Until now the party has kept itself together by holding to a centrist course, refusing to choose between left and right, and affording militants a more effective base from which to pursue their particular goals than was available elsewhere. But in the current context of Chilean politics it will be difficult to continue fulfilling these requirements. The persistence of the three-thirds party system will force the party off the centre and into choosing between centre-left and centre-right alliances.

Party progressives would leap at the chance to embrace the former alternative, particularly if other leftist groups embrace more liberal or democratic Socialist concepts, and even though such a move might alienate substantial numbers of party moderates. The latter, on the other hand, do not wish to provoke an exodus by progressives, as it would leave them less capable of resisting the domination of right-wing groups with which they are not in full agreement. But they appear even less willing to collaborate with a united left that they long have considered their party's principal rival and antagonist.

In these circumstances, the party could split, as in Peru, into rival Christian Democratic organisations: a social Christian party representing entrepreneurial and conservative popular and working-class elements; and a Christian Socialist party backed by progressive intellectuals and younger, more radical workers, peasants, and organised slum dwellers. The two would presumably dispute the patrimony of their common tradition, although neither would enjoy the stature or leverage of the original PDC. Alternatively, party progressives could be absorbed within a unified and a more democratic Socialist party or by a strengthened *Izquierda Cristiana*, leaving the PDC a more coherent but ultimately less attractive force.

Notes

1. Apparently Frei's government looks better in retrospect. In a recent (July 1986) survey of greater Santiago, it received the highest approval rating (5.9 on a scale of 1 to 7) of any government since 1932.

2. The *Movimiento de Accion Popular Unitaria* was formed largely by *rebeldes*. Most *terceristas* remained within the PDC until August 1971 when they left to form the *Izquierda Cristiana*.

3. Surveys taken in Santiago during the last year report extremely low approval (15 per cent to 36 per cent) and support (13 per cent) ratings for General Pinochet.

4. In a July 1986 Gallup poll the Christian Democrats had far and away the most extensive support (40.2 per cent, 62.6 per cent and 15.7 per cent) in those sectors (centre-left, centre, and centre-right) making up the bulk of the electorate.

5. Like the Spanish Communists in the early post-Franco period, the party's current high standing in public opinion polls may by conjunctural, i.e., expressive of the tendency for recently unleashed political forces and energies to fill the channels and vehicles most familiar and most immediately available to them, and not likely to survive its organisational problems and weaknesses.

6. With the party inactive, many of its labour and neighbourhood activists were drawn into organisations and activities sponsored by the Church but open to all popular forces. The experience seems to have strengthened their interest in the unity of popular forces and in their own autonomy vis-a-vis party leaders.

7. Cf. Arturo Valenzuela, 'Origines y Caracteristicas del Sistema de Partidos en Chile: Proposiciòn para Un Gobierno Parlamentario' in *Estudios Publicos* No. 18 (Autumn 1985).

8. Except for the years during which the Communist party was outlawed (1948–58), only one (1965) since 1941 did any of the blocs win more than 44.4 per cent or less than 20 per cent of the total vote in a congressional election.

9. The PDC's attachment to its own 'alternative' project, its disdain for other forces, and its internal divisions have been important factors in the hardening of ideological and political lines.

10. The *Alianza Democratica* brought together Christian Democrats, Radicals,

Liberals, Republicans, Social Democrats, Popular Socialists, and until they withdrew in December 1986 moderate (Nuñez) Socialists. The remaining leftist parties belong to the *Movimiento Democratico Popular*, which advocates more forceful resistance to Pinochet and the exclusion of right-wing forces from any post-military government.

Part IV

Development and Conflict

Peter Hertel

International Christian Democracy (*Opus Dei*)

'WE HAVE the great ambition of sanctifying, Christianising the institutions of peoples, science, culture, civilisation, politics, art, social relations. Everything ought to be Christian, as a collective social expression of the faith of men and as a means to save souls, to sustain them in their faith, to lead them to God'.[1] From: *Crónica, Opus Dei* leaders' journal.

1. THE IRRESISTIBLE RISE OF *OPUS DEI*

Opus Dei (the Work of God) has gradually become a strong backwards-looking force in the Catholic Church. With a judicious strategy[2] developed after the second Vatican council at the Centro Romano di Incontri Sacerdotali (CRIS), the *Opus Dei* priests' centre in Rome, it has proved increasingly successful in winning sympathisers at the top of the Church as well as influence in the Vatican. Unknown to many people, it continues its irresistible rise. In *Camino*, his main work, the Spanish priest Josemaria Escrivá de Balaguer y Albás (1902–75), the founder of the organisation, earnestly counselled his followers to use discretion: 'Perhaps it is not the point of your weapon but at least it is the handle'.[3] The constitutions worked out by Escrivá, which have applied to the secular institute *Opus Dei* since 1950, made secrecy regarding members' names a duty.[4] The statutes of *Opus Dei*,[5] which were issued in 1982 when it was given the hitherto unique status of a personal prelature by the pope, and which Escrivá had prepared in advance, allow this practice of secrecy to continue.

But neither handle nor weapon can be concealed entirely. An indiscretion of 1979 brought to light an unpublished document in which Alvaro del Portillo, the organisation's leader, recommended that the Holy See should make the secular institute a personal prelature 'cum proprio populo', to some ecclesiastico-political advantage. It would be possible for the Holy See 'to enjoy more efficient access to a mobile body of (aptly prepared) priests and laity who would constitute a universally effective spiritual and apostolic ferment in Christian life, above all in society and in vocational life, where it is not often easy nowadays to have an apostolically incisive effect with the means usually available to the Church'.[6] With extraordinary precision, Portillo listed successes to date. In 87 countries *Opus Dei* had altogether 72,375 members. There were members in 479 universities and further education institutes over five continents; in 604 newspapers, journals and scientific publications; in 52 radio and TV corporations and so on; in 38 news and publicity agencies; and in 12 film production and distribution companies.

These numbers have probably risen in the meantime. In West Germany alone, the membership, which was about 700 in the seventies, has more than doubled. *Opus Dei* is most strongly represented in Spain with some 30,000 members, followed by Mexico (7,000) and Italy (5,000).

Unfortunately the document said nothing about the political arenas of the mobile corps, which is working for the Christianisation of the world. We know, however, that in Franco's Spain several ministers were *Opus Dei* members. Today too it was parliamentary members in Western countries. It has often been reported from Chile that the financial circles of *Opus Dei* had considerable influence on the thinking of the dictator Pinochet.

2. SECRECY AND CONCEALMENT

Any outsider who wants to verify information of this kind in *Opus Dei* sources will not be shown statistics but will be referred to the main concern of the Work. Like Jesus in Nazareth, Christians should sanctify their work and mundane life in quite everyday vocations. This religious attitude is unexceptionable. There have always been laypeople concerned with everyday sanctification. Precisely in the decades immediately preceding Escrivá (the Work was founded in 1928), the thought of Nazareth, of the hidden everyday life of Jesus, was revivified. To that extent Escrivá's spiritual initiative may be located in a broad current of contemporay secular devotion. Admittedly, *Opus Dei* stressed something which Vatican II also brought out: the vocation of the laity. Moreover *Opus Dei* members, like all Christians, are entitled to live their religious conviction in secret. But *Opus Dei* as a whole is a mobile corps, an ecclesiastico-political and socially ambitious institution which ought to be interrogated about its goals and its influence. The prelature, however, maintains that it has no secular, and certainly no political ambitions. Its means are, it claims, wholly and exclusively supernatural, spiritual and apostolic.

Radio Vatican itself has contradicted this assertion. It is said to be 'pointless to deny that *Opus Dei* in certain countries exerts considerable influence in political, economic and cultural domains'.[7] Yet *Opus Dei* would object that it is not the organisation but only the individual member who is socially active. His vocation, however, is his private concern in which the organisation does not interfere. As a spiritual structure it serves the supernatural welfare of the member.

Nor does the question of social levels get us any further. The Work often quotes this triad from its spiritual garner: 'To sanctify work, to sanctify oneself in work, and to sanctify others through work'. Does that mean that *Opus Dei* does not include the unemployed and the poor of the Third World, who have no work, and therefore neither influence nor money? Or what proportion do they represent? Anyone who asks such questions would most probably receive this answer: Sociology is inappropriate to the supernatural Work of God, divinely established through Josemaria Escrivá whom God himself chose for the purpose. The supernatural character of *Opus Dei* cannot be reconciled with sociological models. There will be no pandering to such sociological reductionism.

The discussion stops here. Either one accepts the shining image of a purely religious organisation, and then empirical problems are superfluous. Or one continues to ask awkward questions and is rejected as a fit partner for dialogue with *Opus Dei*.

3. A NECESSARY BYWORD

In view of this secretive behaviour, how can an outsider hope to say anything about the organisation? Together with Portillo's writings, constitutions and statutes, other secret papers have come to light.[8] Above all there are the 140 leaders in the internal journal *Crónica*, which is made directly available only to the celibate leadership.[9] Furthermore there are reports and books by former members, which arouse worldwide interest because they usually represent the internal life of the prelature as repressive, with its sinister modes of publicity, forceful indoctrination and rigid censorship. *Opus Dei* rejects these assertions and claims that its members live their lives on a voluntary and individually responsible basis.

What is the reason for these contradictions? Those who exert pressure and those who are under pressure do not experience things thus as long as they accept the rules of the game. They only become really aware that they made their decisions under—possibly massive—pressure when they begin to free themselves from *Opus Dei*. To be sure, it seems illuminating that Escrivá, whose authority in *Opus Dei* remains unquestionable, demands 'sacred compulsion'[10] and 'blind obedience'[11] from his followers.

While there are several descriptions of the internal life of the prelature, there is hardly any information on the members' actual social activities. For the most part, the observer has to rely on chance snippets. He may happen on members whose identity has finally been revealed, on institutions which they founded, and on shady channels into which money disappears. But it is easier to discern ideological structures in official and especially internal texts and in conversations with former members. Even though members, within the 'boundaries decided by the ecclesiastical hierarchy' enjoy 'the same freedom as other Catholic believers',[12] there are distinctive common tenets and practices. All of them practise 'the same spirit and the same exercise of asceticism', and receive 'the same instruction'.[13] The English secular priest Vladimir Felzmann, who belonged to *Opus Dei* for 22 years, especially the authoritative priestly leadership, tells us that '*Opus Dei* itself isn't political'. But the leaders purveyed a 'restrictive' view, a 'preconciliar' mentality and 'an approach to life which then colours your decisions'.[14]

Against this background I shall now try to throw some light on the leadership structure and common mentality of the mobile corps and on its methods of social Christianisation.

4. MALE, CELIBATE AND CLERICAL

Opus Dei sees its spirituality as 'lay'. It is not however a 'spirituality of the laity', but a spirituality of those who exercise a vocation 'in the world'. This brings secular priests into the organisation and ensures the spiritual unity of priests and laity in the corps. The priests play the decisive role in the lay spirituality of *Opus Dei*. The statutes say that the instruction of *Opus Dei* members is the specific concern of priests. As laypeople, future members enter the strictly compartmentalised men's and women's sections, and at the same time make the lifelong decision whether to join the celibate membership (some fifty per cent), or the membership of those who are already married or may marry. If one has been a celibate male lay member of the prelature for some time, one is open to selection for the priesthood and may enter the 'prelature clergy' (1.6 per cent of members), who hold the top offices in *Opus Dei*: prelate, general vicar, priest-secretary of the women's section and regional vicars. Only the clergy are fully integrated in the prelature and are wholly subject to the prelate. The laypeople, on the other hand, are subject to the clergy exercising their office and to their instructions in so far as the aims of the prelature are concerned. Otherwise they remain under the jurisdiction of the diocesan bishop—like the secular priests who have joined *Opus Dei* through the Holy Cross society of priests. A small élite of laymen are also qualified for leadership posts below the top level. They resemble the priests as far as instruction and way of life are concerned.

Unlike the men, women can neither enter the elective structure of *Opus Dei* nor do they possess, as do the men, a committee responsible for the overall conduct of the Work. Their section is controlled by three members of the men's section (prelate, general vicar, priest secretary) and the 'central women's committee'. Celibate women are largely responsible for the domestic work in *Opus Dei* centres.

All this means that in *Opus Dei* actual lay life is structured in accordance with preconciliar norms. In any event, it is not even approximately developed to the extent of many dioceses, whose councils and synods—in accordance with current legislation—not only allow men to debate and to make decisions, but to do so together with women.

5. THE IMMACULATE REMNANT OF THE TRUE CHURCH

Former leading members of *Opus Dei* have referred to an unyielding militancy which sees the organisation as the guardian of truth and Catholics who thinks differently as heretics. This spirit of demarcation was expressed in *Crónica*[15] soon after Vatican II. There the Work is described as 'holy', 'pure' and 'unchangeable'. '*Opus Dei* possesses a divine dynamic character that renews itself continually' (*Crónica* 1968). 'You [*Opus Dei*] are all beautiful and there is no stain in you. The Work is "tota pulchra".' Therefore there is no need for reform of any kind—contrary to the Church. The Work was founded by God to save the Church; and its founder Escrivá, 'El Padre', seems like Jesus, the Good Shepherd: 'Our Father is also the Good Shepherd who leads the flock of the whole Work. ... He spends his life so that we, his children, may have it in greater abundance (*Crónica* 1971)'. Four years after the end of the Council the Father complained of a period of error in the Church, and in 1972 he even said in a leading article in *Crónica*: 'The evil comes from within and from very high up. There is an authentic rottenness, and at times it seems as if the Mystical Body of Christ were a corpse in decomposition, that stinks. How many offences against God there are! We are fragile, and even more fragile than others; but, as I have already said: we have a commitment of Love; we must now give our existence a sense of reparation'.[16]

Even if we remind ourselves that religious writers sometimes take themselves too seriously, there is no doubt that *Opus Dei* sees itself as the sacred, immaculate remnant of the true Church. But Escrivá also detected stains in society which counter the desired Christianisation and have to be removed. The largest stain of all is atheistic Marxism.

6. IN AN IMPERFECT SOCIETY

Opus Dei was formed in a largely closed Catholic country, in the Spain of the nineteen-thirties. At the same time the political and social structure came into being to which the mobile corps is still attached. The Spanish bishops and many Catholics were convinced that the Spanish civil war was not a socio-political confrontation but a religious war between Christianity and Communism, a crusade and an upsurge of brotherly love. When Franco triumphed and Catholicism alongside him, the bishops found themselves on the victors' dias. In *Integrismo católico* they attached themselves to Franco because he made the State a Catholic State.

Even before the civil war, elements of the anti-Communistic élite of the country came together in *Opus Dei*. Peter Berglar, Escrivá's German biographer and himself an *Opus Dei* member, purposefully describes in great detail how Communists looked for the priest Escrivá in order to execute him. They even hanged a man whom they had mistaken for him. According to Berglar, this unfortunate creature is 'an *Opus Dei* martyr in the sight of God'[17]—clearly the only one to date. At any rate we do not know of even a single *Opus Dei* member among the many Christian martyrs of Latin America who are often persecuted as Communist-inclined.

Those civil war experiences would seem to have acted as a kind of key encounter for Escrivá and to have comprised the universal political image for *Opus Dei*. Vladimir Felzmann says of Escrivá: 'The one hatred in his life was Communism: The evil, because he suffered. He was officially killed by Communists'. The dualism 'Communism v. Christianity' must also have determined Escrivá's view of overall European events. Felzmann, who was occasionally a private discussion partner of the Founder, and at his request translated *Camino* into Czech, reports that, even at the end of the nineteen-sixties, Escrivá tried to some extent to excuse Hitler, and even to reduce the enormity of the Holocaust because Hitler by intervening on Franco's behalf saved Christianity in Spain. For Escrivá it was a matter not of 'Hitler against the Jews or Hitler against the Slavs, it was Hitler against Communism'.

In 1959, in his letter *Dei amore*,[18] Josemaria Escrivá spoke of stains which 'smear the world' and prevent its christianisation. 'First there is that red stain [he is referring to atheistic Marxism] which spreads so quickly over the globe, which tears down everything, and which would destroy even the least supernatural spark'. Then there is a liberalising stain: an 'abandoned sensualism, even madness' and finally, a 'stain of a different hue': the suppression in public life of faith and its manifestations'.

Even today the mentality of the foundation period colours specific options supported by the majority. It is interesting that *Opus Dei* politicians whose identities have been revealed, have always belonged to bourgeois, Christian conservative and Fascist parties and groups, and not to Socialist, social democratic, liberal radical-democratic organisations.

7. CHRISTIANISATION FROM ABOVE

In the course of their Christianisation of society, *Opus Dei* members pursue an authoritarian strategy in accordance with the legal and thought structures of the community. They begin at the top, and look for top people whom they can win over, in order to win access to a specific sector from which they slowly but surely work their way downwards. Their statutes require them to exercise their apostolate especially among intellectuals and those holding public office. The constitutions put it even more clearly: 'The characteristic means for the apostolate of the Institute is public office holders: especially those with a directive function'.[19]

This idea is best put into practice in so-called Catholic countries, particularly if the ruling powers there broadcast their claim to combat Marxism or Communism, and to serve Christian faith.

Church politics has habitually concentrated on the particular powers that be and continues to do so. It would even come to terms with Communist leaders. *Opus Dei*, on the other hand, takes the older anti-Communist road. It is no wonder if *Opus Dei* members cannot work with Communist regimes. It is almost unrepresented in Eastern Europe. Attempts to gain a foothold in Poland have obviously proved fruitless.

In Western countries *Opus Dei*—also favoured by the general trend to the right—is moving smoothly ahead. The discreet way in which *Opus Dei* members establish their own connections helps the foundation of a fine basic network of social links. That is why so many people find the Work so sinister. You know that it is there, but who knows where and how. To assess the social strength of the organisation you would need to detect the economic networks above all else. But here the outsider can see little more than outlines.

8. A POVERTY-STRICKEN OPUS DEI WITH CAPITAL

In the formal legal sense, the personal prelature and Escrivá are rather like a poor family with numerous children. But family members, who are almost always unknown, set up companies and banks, institutes and foundations. Felzmann reports that the English *Opus Dei* leaders intended to pay the contributions made to *Opus Dei* to the Netherhall Education Association, a charitable foundation, since its leading members were also *Opus Dei* members, and *Opus Dei* would then be able to use the money for its own purposes.

Whether this system seems appropriate or inappropriate, it has to be studied if any light is to be shed on the complicated cover-ups. One must never forget that the membership of *Opus Dei* has two aspects, a formal and a practical.

Certainly the most important *Opus*-proximate foundation is the Limmat-Stiftung, which was established in Zürich, the international banking centre, in 1972. Latterly it was connected partly in terms of staff and partly in terms of organisation with *Opus*-related banks and foundations and/or banks and foundations directed by *Opus*-members in Spain, Germany and Latin America. Some threads of this network were revealed when the multi-millionaire *Opus* member José María Ruiz Mateos, the leading Spanish private entrepreneur, was dispossessed by the State and was found guilty of defrauding the revenue and of major currency offences. Meanwhile he explained that the leading Spanish *Opus Dei* members Cantero and Montuenga required him—a convinced member—to provide hundreds of millions of pesetas for the apostolic work of *Opus Dei*. He proferred copies of bank documents in evidence.

The Swiss bank of Ruiz Mateos and his multinational Rumasa concern was the Nordfinanzbank in Zürich. At the same time, its managing director, Arthur Wiederkehr (who was partly responsible for laundering the payments through cover firms), with four *Opus Dei* members made up the five-man board of the Limmat Foundation. Wiederkehr and the Nordfinanzbank also had shares in the worldwide banking empire of the Italian Roberto Calvi.

Calvi was the head of the largest Italian private bank, the Banco Ambrosiano, which went spectacularly bankrupt in 1982. Not only the Banco Ambrosiano but the Vatican Bank IOR, because it was by a long way the largest minority shareholder in Ambrosiano, were declared coresponsible by the Italian bank inspectorate. Together with 88 Ambrosiano backers IOR agreed a compromise payment of 250 million dollars, and was able to cut six million for speedy payment.

Whereas these facts are verifiable, one question has remained unanswered: How could the money be obtained so quickly? The explanation is that *Opus*

Dei financial circles also came to the rescue, but required the Holy See to assign to them the decisive influence on Vatican politics as against Communist States and third-world States. This assertion accords with statements made by the family of Calvi, who lost his life in circumstances as yet unexplained, and by the former industrialist Ruiz Mateo.

Opus Dei has rejected any claim that it participated in such affairs with the now almost stereotyped statement that it is a purely religious institution and that it is not active in an economico-financial sense. Moreover its member Ruiz Mateos falsified the facts.

9. INTEGRALISM AS A KEY

It seems permissible to describe the division of the world and the individual into two closed realms—supernature and nature—as an *Opus Dei* ruse to stifle uncomfortable questions. But the problem goes deeper. As early as 1963 the theologian Hans Urs von Balthasar characterised this attitude as integralism, when he also called *Opus Dei* the 'strongest integralist power complex in the Church'.[20]

Because of its complexity, here we can only touch on the question of integralism as the key to a theological understanding of *Opus Dei*. In the integralist conception, the self-contained realm of the supernatural dominates the world of nature. Integralists, who gravitate to the supernatural realm, consider that they are in possession of the truth.

There are many integralist phenomena in *Opus Dei*: the practices are largely secret: 'sacred compulsion' and 'blind obedience' are expected. Whoever criticizes the Work must expect to be classified as an imperceptive know-all or even a slanderer. The supernatural must also dominate society. Everything is to be Christianised—as a collective social expression of human faith. This would be the baptism of society, where no room would remain for philosophic and highly-refined, pluriform political viewpoints.

The essential mentality behind these demarcations may be discerned in the conception of *Opus Dei*, which is in fact only one Church group among many, as sacred, unchangeable, immaculate, immortal and divine: a claim which appertains in any case to the Church as a whole. Criticism of *Opus Dei* is often equated with criticism of the Church pure and simple. If however a single group is identified with the welfare of the Church or the welfare of the Church with itself, then the permissible multiplicity of spiritualities and modes of belief, of cultural, social and political traditions, and of theological schools, is called in question. New groups in the Church are inclined to isolate themselves and to elevate themselves above others. But the exclusivity of *Opus Dei* leads precisely to a monolithic Church and to spiritual and practical intolerance.

Escrivá's Work is so strong in a church-political sense and economically too, that we are forced to live with it in the long term. Its religious gravity can be a critical challenge to all Christians: Do they allow the famous 'Aggiornamento' to descend to the level of mere adaptation? Do they understand being a Christian as an inclusive everyday task? But that is not all. The organisation is also concerned to acquire bastions of power within the Church and to reverse the new beginnings of theology in this century, especially after Vatican II. Its members try to promote christianisation in association with power and capital and through economic manipulation.

The mobile corps has increasingly become a special instrument for the spiritual and institutional rectification of the Church, with all the negative consequences of such a procedure for the individual but also for the credibility of the Church itself.

Translated by J. G. Cumming

Notes

1. *Crónica*, 1963, No. 8 (see 9 below).

2. The nature of this article does not allow me to discuss strategy in greater detail. Interested readers are referred to: Peter Hertel *'Ich verspreche euch den Himmel'. Geistlicher Anspruch, gesellschaftliche Ziele und kirchliche Bedeutung des Opus Dei* (Düsseldorf 1985) pp. 123–142.

3. Josemaria Escrivá de Balaguer *Camino* (Madrid 41st ed. 1984) p. 192, No. 655.

4. *Constitutiones Societatis Sacerdotalis Sanctae Crucis et Operis Dei* (Rome 1950), Pars II, Caput III, No. 190 *seq.* (may be consulted in author's library).

5. *Codex Iuris Particularis Operis Dei* (Rome 1982). In accordance with Titulus III, Caput I, No. 899 par. 2, only the diocesan bishop has the right to request the names of some members who are active in his diocesan territory: priests of the prelature and leaders of *Opus Dei* centres. The names of other members (even secular priests associated with *Opus Dei*) must not be disclosed (Codex may be consulted in author's library).

6. Alvaro del Portillo (e Javier Echevarria) *Trasformazione dell' Opus Dei in Prelatura Personale* (Rome, 23 April 1979), 1, 99 (to be consulted in author's library).

7. Heinrich Segur *Orden stellen sich vor*, Radio Vatican, German Section (4 September 1979).

8. Giancarlo Rocca *'L'Opus Dei'*, *Appunti e Documenti per una Storia* (Rome 1985) offers 53 partly secret documents (192–203).

9. The Oxford lecturer John J. Roche, before leaving *Opus Dei*, copied some 140 'Crónica' leaders in an English translation provided by *Opus Dei*. (Copies may be consulted in author's library).

10. *Camino*, p. 115, No. 387.

11. *Op. cit.*, p. 282, No. 941.
12. *Codex*, No. 109.
13. *Op. cit.*, No. 6.
14. All Felzmann quotations come from an interview which he authorised: Hertel (footnote 2) pp. 192–212.
15. The following *Crónica* quotations are from leaders of the years 1968–71.
16. *Crónica*, No. 2, 1972. As Opus Dei in Germany asserts in a *Crónica* 'report', which was to appear two months after Escrivá's leader in No. 4 (1972). The quotation continues thus after the words 'in foul decay'; 'But do not be afraid. I said: *it seems.*' According to Felzmann the 'Report' quotation is not an original quotation from Escrivá. In about 1975 offensive sections were removed from *Crónica* and new pages were worked in. Whether the *Report* appears on one of the new-for-old pages, or whehter Escrivá is reported here indirectly, is something I cannot investigate because I cannot check *Crónica*.
17. Peter Berglar *Opus Dei. Leben und Werk des Gründers Josemaria Escrivá* (Salzburg 1983) p. 148.
18. Cited after Berglar, p. 125.
19. *Constitutiones*, No. 202.
20. Hans Urs von Balthasar *Integralismus: Wort und Wahrheit*, 18, (Freiburg, December 1963) 742.

Otto Maduro

Christian Democracy and the Liberating Option for the Oppressed in Latin American Catholicism

1. INTRODUCTION

IN LATIN America, with the majority of the population being Catholic, Christian Democracy has often presented itself as the only, or at least the best political choice for Catholics. Does such a claim make any sense in 1987? In only two Latin American countries—El Salvador and Guatemala—have Christian Democrat parties recently gained power through elections (elections in which the political organisations of the Socialist Left played no part). In two others—Chile and Venezuela—the Christian Democrats have held political power in the recent past and can reasonably expect to do so again in the near future. There are, perhaps, only four among the other twelve nations of the continent in which Christian Democracy has any importance in the national, social and political spectrum.

Meanwhile, a great variety of other forms of participating in social and political life—different from and even opposed to Christian Democracy—have come to gain favour with an increasing number of Catholics in Latin America. 'Christian Left' groups, 'Camilista' (after Camilo Torres) groups, 'Christians for Socialism' and several other movements have preceded—sometimes with no later connection—liberation theology and the base Christian communities. Various Social Democratic parties—those in Chile, Venezuela, El Salvador and Nicaragua, amongst others—have gone through internal divisions caused by the rise—within them—of radical currents of Catholic-social thought. Finally, large numbers of Latin American believing

Catholics (above all in the lower and middle strata of the population) are becoming steadily more organised in leagues, groups, networks, movements and parties distinct from—and often opposed to—the Christian Democrat parties and unions, in order to pursue their aims.

So what relationship—historical, social, political and cultural—exists in Latin America between Christian Democracy, on the one hand, and, on the other, those other means of social and political Catholic commitment which some would call 'radical', 'Socialist', 'leftist' or, more recently, 'liberating'? In the following few pages I am going to essay a reply (partial, partisan, conjectural and provisional) to this question. A reply consciously made from a particular viewpoint: that of a Latin American lay Catholic Socialist (ex-Christian Democrat)—from the Caribbean and Venezuela, to give more detail—forty-two years old, a philosopher and religious sociologist, deeply identified with the spirit blowing in theologies of liberation.

2. EUROPEAN CATHOLICISM AND LATIN AMERICAN CHRISTIAN DEMOCRACY

Perhaps the first characteristic of Latin American Christian Democracy that needs pointing out is its European and Catholic origins. Like many other facets of Latin American society and politics, Christian Democracy originated largely beyond the frontiers of the New World: mainly in Western European Catholic thought since the second World War. In Europe, as later in Latin America, Christian Democracy is a political (not ecclesiastical) movement, secular (not clerical), but one which arose from ecclesiastical initiatives, organisations and concerns strongly influenced by the clergy. European Christian Democracy took shape in a weakened Church, weakened first by the loss of the rising middle classes and, later, of the growing working classes. A Church which felt threatened both by the liberal anti-clericism of the middle classes and by Socialist rejection of religion. A Church, therefore, on the defensive against both the ruling capitalism and emerging Socialism. A Church that dreamt of the past, barely tolerated the present and feared the uncertain future.

Something similar happened also in the Latin American Church. A new model of the Church, of which Christian Democracy is, in a way, a manifestation came into being in post-War European Catholicism. This is what has been called the 'New Christendom' programme, which is opposed to—but at the same time near to and supportive of—both the totalitarian ideal of restoring medieval Christendom and the dominant liberal model of Western Europe. This model of New Christendom—sanctioned by the 'social teaching of the Church' through the social encyclicals from *Rerum Novarum* of Leo XIII (1891) to those of John XXIII—has found enemies both inside and outside the Catholic Church, first in Europe and later in Latin America: inside, in the old Catholic aristocracy which saw ideas such as New Christendom, Integral Humanism, Catholic Action and Christian Democracy as dangerous concessions to liberal-bourgeois atheism; outside, in the anti-clerical middle class, working class and Socialist elites, who saw the same ideas as a clerical conspiracy designed to restore the old power of the Church.

European Christian Democracy grew—slowly and with difficulty—from the end of the nineteenth century to the period after the second World War as the political expression of this 'New Chistendom' programme. In Latin America it followed the same path after the 1929 crisis. An influential sector of the Catholic laity used Christian Democracy as the vehicle for pursuing their aim of becoming active protagonists of the Church and of society or, at least, active protagonists of the Church in the political life of society. This happened first in Western Europe and later in Latin America, but in both cases it involved the White, urban, adult, masculine, intellectual and upwardly mobile Catholic middle classes. This sociological profile gave Christian Democracy, at the time of its struggle for power, a tense—and often conflictive—relationship with the clergy on one side (especially with the more conservative popes and bishops) and with the most powerful groups in society on the other (particularly dictators and big landowners, more so if these were not Catholics, and unless a greater 'common enemy' impelled Christian Democracy to ally itself to these other enemies).

In this way Christian Democracy was able to put forward—from its tense distance from the conservative clergy, the aristocracy, the army, the bourgeoisie and the anti-clerical intellectuals—the Utopia of a new society: the communitarian society of Integral Humanism, a third way between Capitalism and Socialism. While Christian Democracy remained a minority opposition grouping (i.e. till the late forties in Western Europe and the sixties in Latin America) this Utopia could function as a magnet drawing certain sectors of the proletariat, bourgeoisie and intellectuals among Catholics, the middle classes (including non-Catholics) and the peasants. Its lack of any socio-economic analysis of Capitalism and of definite and specific political programmes, enabled each sector to understand this third way in a manner suited to its own social position and to entertain hopes from it accordingly. So, for some, the Social Democrat programme was that of legal, gentle, peaceful, moderate Socialism, one that would respect the position of religion; for others, on the other hand, it represented a Capitalism of small businesses, social services and harmony between investors and workers; for others, again, it evoked a corporative theocracy, a sort of 'new middle ages'. These differences, however, were submerged or minimised in the face of Christian

Democracy's general opposition to monarchy, dictatorship, high Capitalism and atheist Socialism in both Europe and Latin America.

3. LATIN AMERICAN CHRISTIAN DEMOCRACY: ROOTS AND PROMISES

The spread of liberal thought and Capitalist economics in Latin America from the end of the last century led to the development of many 'problems' similar to those which the Church had faced in Europe during the same—or earlier—decades. The Catholic clergy of Latin America—European, educated in Europe or by Europeans, and dependent on European ecclesiastical authorities—then tended, when faced with such 'problems' to repeat the *European solution* from the thirties: lining up Catholic lay people (above all White, urban, masculine, educated and upwardly mobile middle class lay people) in Catholic Action organisations, controlled by the Church hierarchy, educating them in the social teaching of the Church and encouraging them to bring about a New Christendom from their intellectual, professional and political positions in civil society.[1]

Of course, as usually happens, the form, content and consequences of this ecclesiastical policy varied enormously between one Latin American country and another. Particularly since the second World War, this policy has led to the formation of Christian Democratic parties in several Latin American countries, but not in all. There are also significant differences between these parties, both in their history and their consequences. Almost all started out as '*Catholic* parties' and sometimes—as in Venezuela from 1946 to 1964— claiming to be the only Catholic party. Their founders were generally young Catholics from the White, urban, rising middle classes, militants in Catholic Action, who had studied in religious schools and colleges, and then followed careers in the Humanities, generally in Law. Their ideology—drawn from Spanish translations of Jacques Maritain, Luigi Sturzo, Joseph Folliet, the Malines Codices and the social encyclicals—hardly ever introduced any innovation on its European sources.

This *Catholic* character developed in clear opposition to *laicism*: a rabid, liberal, anti-clericalism which led, in several Latin American countries, to a persecution of the Church by the new elites in power. This laicism (inherited from the wars of independence against Spain in the nineteenth century) took new shape in liberal, democratic and/or populist programmes in the first half of the twentieth century as a genuine political laicism: an attempt to eliminate all Church influence in administering society, putting the Church in a position of total subordination to the liberal-bourgeois State. So it was also as opposition to this political laicism that Christian Democracy developed—

often out of the old conservative parties—as 'the Catholic party'. This determined many of its later alliances, dilemmas and conflicts.

As long as they remained outside State power, fighting against those who held it at the time, the Christian Democrat parties in several countries of Latin America played a strongly critical and, at times, even radical role. As in some countries of Western Europe, this often attracted large sectors of the working and peasant classes, which strengthened the tendencies opposing national, multi-national and United States Capitalism, tendencies widely represented in Latin American Christian Democracy. The struggles against military dictatorships, landowning oligarchies and extreme right-wing groups—which also characterised anti-Fascist resistance in Europe—deepened the Utopic dimension of Latin American Christian Democracy. This—it has to be said— often led to conflicts between Latin American Christian Democracy and its European forerunners.[2]

At the same time, fear of Communism (based on religious reasons as strong as, or stronger than, class motives) developed, just as in Western Europe after the War, as the central leitmotiv of nearly all the Latin American Christian Democrat parties, more so in countries where, and at times when, Socialist ideas and organisations were receiving strong support from workers, students and/or—eventually—peasants. This anti-Communism often made Christian Democracy attractive to sectors of the middle classes and the better off among the Latin American population, sectors (often anti-clerical) whose motivations and hopes were not only different from, but opposed to, those who supported Christian Democracy, because they saw it as a revolutionary and liberating force.

Various factors contributed to the emergence of Christian Democracy as a popular alternative in several countries of Latin America: the failure of 'traditional' Capitalism, the fears and hopes generated by the Cuban revolution; the response of the first Catholic president of the USA, John F. Kennedy, with his promises of the Alliance for Progress and the Peace Corps; and, undoubtedly, the call of the new Pope, John XXIII, for the Church to play an active role in the struggle for peace and social justice.

The developmentist theory counted on very wide support at this time (except among those on the extreme right and left wings). Latin American Christian Democracy embraced this theory enthusiastically and devoted itself completely to the idea of outright development. Backwardness and the past then looked like the main enemies. Modernisation and the future were seen optimistically as a promise soon to be achieved. In this climate the objective seemed obvious, and criticism of injustice became easy and almost natural.

So, in Chile in 1964 in Venezuela in 1968, two Latin American Christian Democrat parties had—for the first time—the experience of their Western

European precursors two decades before: they won democratic elections (against both left and right). They then found that they had to demonstrate that their 'third alternative' that of a 'revolution in freedom' was viable. But they also—and this proved more difficult still—found themselves urged to satisfy the contradictory hopes that their vague, ambiguous and optimistic message had aroused in the heterogeneous electoral base which had led them both to power.

4. LATIN AMERICAN CHRISTIAN DEMOCRACY: THE FAILURE OF POWER

Once in political power, Christian Democracy had to face up to the hard realities, contradictory pressures and difficult moral dilemmas of capitalism in Latin America, which was characterised by dependency and 'under-development'. Faced with the ambiguity of real power—as had previously happened in Europe—the characteristic features of Christian Democracy proved of little use. These features might be described as: (a) its refusal to recognise the social reality as conflictive and its conviction that harmony between the social classes—and between the third world and the great powers or, at least, the capitalist great powers—is perfectly possible and, indeed, normal; (b) the virtual complete separation between the principles it preached and the policies it practised, added to the frequent lack of specific alternative programmes for coping with the wide-spread poverty and dependency typical of Latin American societies; (c) the predominance of middle-class professional people and intellectuals more attuned to and identified with the bourgeoisie than the popular classes in the ranks of its party officials and government ministers; (d) its refusal, finally, to recognise the corrupting influence of power, money and the individualistic and consumerist values of Capitalism, together with its ingenuous conviction that the political-religious faith of Christian Democracy is enough in itself to overcome such difficulties.

With these features Christian Democracy began to tackle the opposing demands of the labour and management sectors with regard to taxes, public spending, official policies on employment, wages and prices, health, education, housing, communications and other public services. Often the solution that suited the managers was harmful to the workers and the unemployed, and vice versa and—contrary to the theoretical dreams of Christian Democracy—finding a solution satisfactory to both sides was often impossible. The business sector—closer to the leadership of the Christian Democrats, armed with more powerful resources for putting pressure on them and with greater experience in dealing with political and government bureaucracy—generally gained the upper hand. Much the same happened with the conflicting requirements of the leadership (political, military, financial, business, commercial and cultural) of the United States, on the one hand, and the nationalist sectors of the Latin American countries, on the other.

The post-War period of growth was drawing to its end, which meant that the huge expectations aroused by Christian Democrats among the poor—and among Catholic Activists committed to them—were almost immediately frustrated. Many people began to look for alternatives to Christian Democracy. Furthermore, the gradual disappearance of anti-clericalism from other political areas did away with the pretensions of Christian Democrats to be the only Catholic presence in politics.

But—unlike the classic 'right' and, above all, unlike right-wing dictatorships—Christian Democrats sought (as in Europe) to go on winning democratic elections, elections which they preached as the only legitimate title for exercising political power. Because of this—and also because of other internal and external requirements of legitimacy—Christian Democracy had to try to satisfy, at least minimally, the demands of the majority, that is of the workers and the unemployed.

So what the 'third way' of Christian Democracy produced once in power—in Chile, Venezuela and now in El Salvador—was a moderated dependent Capitalism, similar to that produced earlier in Italy, West Germany and Belgium. A system of neo-liberal government which, faced with the demands made upon it by proprietors on one side and the proletariat on the other, tried to follow a policy of partial and unequal satisfaction of these demands: the more powerful were the more satisfied, the weakest the least satisfied. But, in the end, nobody—outside the leaders of the party and the government and a few small sectors of the middle classes—was really happy. A system of government within the orbit of the United States: not always sufficiently submissive to gain the confidence of the United States leadership, but sufficiently dependent to become a key piece in United States policy towards Latin America and, therefore, incapable of inspiring confidence in the more nationalist sectors of Latin American politics.

Christian Democracy suffered from the self-deception (common on the left as well) of believing that on 'taking power' radical change would immediately be possible. When this was not achieved, instead of keeping its sights set on the horizon of a definite utopia (which would have served to criticise, correct and guide specific policies in the direction of long-term change) Christian Democracy progressively lowered its sights to mere pragmatic exercise of power, keeping its utopia on the level of a purely formal (empty) declaration of abstract principles.

Moderate doctrinal opposition to national and multi-national Capitalism then gave way—with Christian Democrats in political power—to a deep adaptation to Capitalism. So Christian Democracy began to show its inability to be a 'third way' between Capitalism and Socialism. The experiences in Chile, Venezuela and El Salvador—like those of Italy, West Germany and Belgium—did show Christian Democracy to be a mediating and moderating force in the conflicts between labour and capital, but a force operating from within the limits and on the side of capital. Its anti-Socialist dimension, furthermore, has gradually grown out of all proportion to the point where large sectors of Latin American Christian Democrats now prefer dictatorships of the right—like that of Pinochet and others—to democratic social experiments like that of Popular Unity and the Sandinista Front.[3]

5. THE CHURCH IN LATIN AMERICA: BEYOND CHRISTIAN DEMOCRACY

The 'developmentist' policy backed by the Kennedy administration for Latin America in the sixties—and very closely followed by the Catholic Church and by Social Democrat, Christian Democrat and liberal governments of the continent—resulted in complete failure. Economic dependency, inflation, unemployment, malnutrition, illiteracy, concentration of capital in the hands of a few, the growing poverty of the majority, internal conflicts and massive emigration increased instead of decreasing, and frustration led to increasing protest by the oppressed against the 'solutions' put forward by various forms of Capitalism in Latin America (including the 'third Way' of Christian Democracy).

Faced with this deteriorating situation Christian Democracy proved incapable of providing solutions while in government, and equally incapable of putting forward credible solutions while in opposition. Caught between concern for the poverty of the workers and fear of the growing wave of protest (strikes, demonstrations, seizures of factories, land, houses and foodstuffs, the growth of trade unions and left-wing parties, etc.) by the workers against their poverty, Christian Democracy has tended to be led more by fear than by solidarity with the working classes. So repression against popular protest (while in government) and tolerance of the growing number of anti-Communist dictatorships (while in opposition) have been the reactions of Christian Democracy in Latin America when the oppressed have risen up as active social agents, making Christian Democracy progressively a force inimical to the emergent popular movements.

In the Catholic Church, meanwhile, an official critique of Capitalism has been developing, going far beyond the Christian Democrat position both in theory and in practice. From *Mater et Magistra* (1961) and *Pacem in Terris* (1963), on through the documents of the second Vatican Council (1965) to

Populorum Progressio (1967) there is a steady line of innovation which contributed to free the creative spirit of the Church in Latin America with regard to Catholic social teaching.[4]

This creativity has become the official voice of Latin American Catholicism, particularly since the second General Conference of the Latin American Episcopate held at Medellín in Colombia in 1968 and the third held at Puebla in Mexico in 1979. The main impulses for this creativity have been the base Christian communities and the theology of liberation.

This creativity has evoked positive responses from the Holy See (apart from the negative ones which have also undeniably been produced) from the encyclical *Evangelii Nuntiandi* (1965) by Paul VI up to the recent Letter of John Paul II to the Bishops' Conference of Brazil, not to mention the same pope's encyclical *Laborem Exercens* (1981) and the Vatican *Instructions* (1984 and 1986) dealing with the theology of liberation.

As has happened with many other movements in history, Christian Democracy, which was originally in the vanguard of the Church from which it sprang, has moved—and not only in Latin America—to the rearguard of Catholicism. It has—putting it metaphorically—remained at the gates of the Vatican and of Medellín. In a sense 1968 marks the break between Christian Democracy and the Catholic Church in Latin America. The Church has increasingly seen and welcomed the emergence, within it and in society, of popular classes as *agents* of their own history, allowing itself to be challenged and transformed by this incursion of the poor. The 'preferential option for the poor', commitment to the liberation of the oppressed, increasingly marks contemporary Latin American Catholicism. Christian Democracy, on the other hand, has held out against doing the same, victim—amongst other things—of the inertia and fears of its ageing leadership.

Because of this, and for other reasons, Christian Democracy has lost the prophetic, innovative, critical and utopic strength which it had at various times during the first half of the twentieth century. Its repeated failure in government with the resulting 'ideological emptying' which has characterised Latin American Christian Democracy over the past two decades, has made it lose any credibility it might have had among the people and progressive Catholics. So the Christian Democrat leadership seems to be left with no other motive for action than worldly temptations to power itself, and with no other means of capturing the popular vote than the creation of a 'saleable' image through publicity campaigns.

6. NEW ACTORS, NEW CONFLICTS, NEW RESPONSES

Both inside and outside Christian Democracy many lay Catholic activists—

and several priests and religious also—have, since the early sixties, begun to live and work among the oppressed (often in order to 'stem the Communist advance'). Their actual experience of real human lives and of the efforts, sufferings, hopes, failures and disasters of the oppressed led many of these activitists to a different vision of poverty from that previously prevailing in the Church and in Christian Democracy: a more structural and historic vision, more critical and radical, more conflictive and complex, in solidarity with and committed to poverty. This vision was then nourished with translations into Spanish of new Catholic thought coming from France (Mounier, Lepp, Lebret, Teilhard, Cardonnel, Blanquart, etc.) and from the Vatican.

This led to a multiplication of initiatives aimed at producing active Christian solidarity with the oppressed (within Christian Democracy these were carried out by organisations of the Lay Apostolate, by religious institutions and in the homes and work places of Catholic activists). There were Reviews such as *Christianity and Revolution* edited in Buenos Aires by the Lay Catholic Juan García Elorrio. There were groups of priests committed to the poor, such as ONIS in Peru; there were political-religious revolutionary organisations such as the 'Peoples' United Front' led by Fr Camilo Torres in Colombia. There were educational initiatives aimed at liberating the oppressed, such as 'Popular Action' where Paulo Freire began his experiments in 'conscientisation'. Bishops such as Leonidas Proaño in Riobamba (Ecuador) and Sergio Méndez Arceo in Cuernavaca (Mexico) began to preach a new type of homily and books such as *Development Without Capitalism* by the Chileans Julio Silva Solar and Jacques Chonchol—still then Christian Democrats—had a profound effect.

Of course these sorts of initiatives always brought reactions. On the one hand were simple Catholics from among the people who found the words and solidarity necessary to confirm and articulate their intuitions and hopes, and were thereby encouraged in their struggle for justice. On the other hand were the fears and threats of the ecclesiastical hierarchy, of the Christian Democrat leadership, of government and security authorities, and worse still (especially since Medellín): torture, assassinations, exile and other forms of repression.

Little by little, above all from 1966 to the present day, a growing number of Catholics—from the popular classes or committed to them—began to employ new modes of thought, expression, communication, organisation, struggle, celebration and prayer. An extraordinary variety of forms of participation by Latin American Catholics in the conflictive reality of our societies has developed completely outside Christian Democracy or even in conflict with it: Neighbourhood movements, mothers' groups, family committees for prisoners and 'disappeared', collective market gardens and markets, bible study groups, music groups, sporting teams, trade unions, peasants' leagues, literacy centres, popular feminine circles, etc.

In these forms of participation the people are expressing themselves and developing as the conscious, autonomous and transforming agents of their own history. They are agents, at the same time, of their society and of their church. Without being strictly political, these types of popular organisation undoubtedly have political implications: amongst other things, they threaten the political initiative and monopoly of the most powerful groups and parties.

At the same time, there have been 'left-wing' splits in several Christian Democrat parties of Latin America: the Christian Left and MAPU in Chile, the Christian Left in Venezuela, the revolutionary social-Christian movements in El Salvador and Nicaragua, etc. In Chile there was the Christians for Socialism movement which spread throughout virtually the whole Catholic world with the assassination of Salvador Allende and which today survives only outside Latin America. There were also 'camilistas', groups which formed after the death of Fr Camilo Torres as a guerrilla (15 February 1966 in Colombia), which lasted till the early seventies. Less well known, but no less real, are various other groups of 'progressive' lay Catholics and pastoral workers which have multiplied throughout Latin America over the past twenty years. Many of these movements have disappeared, but their legacy—including many of their original members—is still present in the present liberating option for the oppressed which is a dominant sign of the life of the churches in Latin America in the eighties.

Facing up to oppression and repression, many Latin American Christians have found Marxists sharing similar sufferings, fears, hopes and joys. This meeting—at bottom more practical than theoretical—has helped Marxists to a fresher, deeper and more respectful view of religious faith. At the same time, it has awakened a great interest in Marxism and a deep respect for Marxists in many Christians. Reciprocal tensions and criticisms have not vanished but, increasingly, they seem to be tensions and criticisms within a deep mutual respect and in the context of a partially common struggle.

All these developments in the churches of Latin America have broken the hold of the great powers on the continent. The Rockefeller and Rand Reports (1968 and 1969) indicated fears felt in the United States at this evolution of Latin American Catholicism. Then the Banzer Plan (1972) and the Santa Fe Document (1980) set out an explicit and coherent policy opposed to the option of the Latin American Church for the oppressed. While a 'base ecumenism' identified with this liberating option for the oppressed was spreading, the power groups were implementing policies of weakening, division and repression of those churches that refused to give in to power while, at the same time, applying policies of reinforcement, financial aid and multiplication of those that did. Since Puebla and the Sandinista revolution the fears of those in power have been confirmed and their activities against the liberating commitment of the churches multiplied. Christian Democracy, meanwhile, has been seen more and more as just one alternative party within Latin American dependent capitalism and, therefore, just another instrument of US policy in Latin America.

7. BRIEF PROVISIONAL CONCLUSIONS

The last twenty-five years have been marked by deep and growing changes in the relationship between Catholicism and politics in Latin America. These changes, whose roots are many and complex, can be summed up (without reducing them to this) as the emergence of the oppressed sectors of the population as historical protagonists, as creative agents, effective actors in the life of society and of the Church. Put in another way (and taking into account the influence of production growth, the spread of the communications media, experiences of political democracy, the Catholic *aggiornamento* opened up by John XXIII, etc.), the oppressed peoples of Latin America are losing the passive patience, submissive hope and fatalist inertia to which they have, so many times, been reduced during the past five centuries.

This transformation—in which the base Christian communities and liberation theology constitute an important dimension—has brought about a crisis in the 'traditional' forms of relationship between Church and State on the continent.

When the pastoral actions of the Church—including those carried out by the ecclesiastical hierarchy—are increasingly marked by the needs of the oppressed, then the Church distances itself from power: those in power (economic, political or military) trust the Church as an ally less and less; the Church, correspondingly, sees those in power less and less as protectors or privileged exercisers of Christian faith. This distancing undoubtedly increases the strength and credibility of the Church among the oppressed and lends greater power to the hopes and struggles of the oppressed for their own liberation. But, at the same time, this process stimulates repression against the liberating actions of the Church by those in power.

In this context, Christian Democracy finds itself on the defensive and in retreat. For Christians, *as Christians*, Christian Democracy means nothing more than one of the alternatives available within the Capitalist system—whether they see it as a desirable alternative or criticise it as undesirable. This means that Christian Democracy has ceased to have any Christian meaning. Those Christians who vote for Christian Democrat parties do so, increasingly, out of pragmatic political considerations (including those cases, as in Chile, where 'left-wing' Christians have attached themselves to the Christian Democrats) and *not* for properly 'Christian' reasons. Christian Democracy, for its part, has correspondingly abandoned the theological and political Church-State dialogue which it hoped to open up in the first half of this century; its words and actions relate increasingly less to the *Christian* inspiration from which it originated.

Christian Democracy is still an electoral option in, perhaps, a fifth of the countries of Latin America. Even in these, however, the political actions of the Christian Democrats seem to have nothing to do with any specifically Christian reference.

Since the middle sixties, a *new participant and a new debate* have appeared on the Latin American scene. This participant consists in the emergent popular classes as historical protagonist; and the new debate is that of the active participation of these classes in their own process of liberation. The base Christian communities and liberation theology are an active and creative part of both the debate and the participant. The rise of the protagonist-people and the debate over their liberation have given rise to, amongst other things, a questioning of the traditional activities of the political parties (including those of the Marxist left) and of the churches (including the Catholic Church). Here too, the base Christian communities and liberation theology have played an active and creative part.

In the whole of this process—which Christian Democracy has not even recognised—one of the dimensions that has become apparent is a new way of understanding relations between faith and politics. The predominant tendency in the whole of the Latin American liberation theology movement is not to reduce itself to a purely political movement nor to sacralise a specific political action. Liberation theology is not a political party, new or old, nor does it set out to be one. Liberation theology is not seeking to reproduce the experience of Christian Democracy, that of being the political appendage of the Church, even though one has to recognise that some left-wing Christian groups in Latin America have taken this line, but it has had less effect and lasted less time than Christian Democracy.

Liberation theology then is not a 'political theology', but a theological reflection from which politics too are critically analysed. Nor is it a 'theology of the world', but a theology from which the structures of the real world are also criticised. Liberation theology seeks to be a reflection in faith from the experience of liberation of the oppressed and, from there, to encourage— among many other things that are not directly or strictly 'political'—a flexible plurality of critically chosen political commitments. In other words, liberation theology seeks to be an instrument enabling Christians in the midst of the experience of liberating the oppressed, and in the service of this liberation, to make decisions, find nourishment and critically examine the whole of their personal lives, including their decision-making and their own political commitment.

Translated by Paul Burns

Notes

1. P. Trigo '¿Doctrina Social de la Iglesia? Sí, Pero,¿qué es eso?' in *Nueva Sociedad* 36 (1978) 35–44.
2. A. Sosa and P. E. Gómez 'La Democracia Cristiana en el mundo. Análisis de la VI Conferencia Mundial' in *SIC* 383 (1976) 100–103, 137–144.
3. F. Hinkelammert 'Socialdemocracia y Democracia Cristiana: las reformas y sus limitaciones' in *El juego de los reformismos frente a la Revolución en Centroamérica* ed. H. Assman (San José de Costa Rica, 1981) pp. 13–56.
4. L. Ugalde 'El pensamiento de inspiración cristiana. Su evolución y sus diversas tendencias' (Caracas, documents of the Congress to mark the Bicentenary of the Liberator, on Latin American political thought, 1983) 73pp in TS.

Contributors

WALTER DIRKS was born in Dortmund Hörde in 1901. He studied theology, sociology and philosophy at Paderborn, Münster, Frankfurt and Giessen. From 1924 to 1934 he was arts editor of the 'left-wing' Catholic *Rhein-Mainische Volkszeitung*. In 1933 the Nazis placed him under 'protective custody'. From 1935 to 1943 he worked on the features section of the old *Frankfurter Zeitung*. In 1946, together with Eugen Kogon, he started the *Frankfurter Hefte*. From 1956 to 1967 he directed the cultural department of West German radio. Since his retirement he has been a freelance writer and lives at Wittnau near Freiburg-im-Breisgau. Among his major publications are: *Erbe und Aufgabe* (1931), *Die zweite Republik* (1947), *Die Antwort der Mönche* (1952), *Das schmutzige Geschäft* (1964), *Der singende Stotterer* (1983), *War ich ein linker Spinner?* (1983), *Die Samariter und der Mann aus Samaria* (1985). An eight-volume edition of his collected works is in preparation.

MICHAEL FLEET gained a PhD at the University of California, Los Angeles in 1971 and is now associate professor of Political Science, Marquette University, Milwaukee, Wisconsin. He has written on Christian Democracy, the Latin American Church, and Christian-Marxist relations. His publications include *The Rise and Fall of Chilean Christian Democracy* (1985); 'The Catholic Church and Revolution Struggle in Central America' in *Social Text*, No. 7 (February 1983); 'Neo Conservatism in Latin America' in *Neo-Conservatism: A Social and Religious Phenomenon*, ed. G. Baum and J. Coleman (1981).

PETER HERTEL was born in 1937. He studied Catholic theology in Münster and in Munich and became a journalist. He spent nine years as a national political editor, including a period with the Catholic weekly *Publik*. Since 1973 he has been the 'religion and society' editor of North German Radio. He is a lay apostolate committee member. After many years of research he published a book on the claims of Opus Dei: *'Ich verspreche euch den Himmel'. Geistlicher Anspruch, gesellschaftliche Ziele und kirchliche Bedeutung des Opus Dei* (1985). He has published other works: for instance, on German Catholicism and politics (1975) and on political theology and basic-church initiatives (1982).

FRANZ HORNER, after training in manual skills and passing the Matura in Salzburg, studied economics and social science at the University of Fribourg in Switzerland and political science and philosophy at the John Hopkins University in Bologna and Washington DC between 1958 and 1964. He was then scientific assistant at EFTA and collaborator at the International Centre for Research into Fundamental Questions in Economics at Salzburg. From 1967 to 1976, he was an assistant at the Institute of Political Science at the University of Salzburg, where he passed the Habilitation in 1973 and was appointed Professor of Political Theory and the History of Ideas in 1976. His publications include: *Die sozialen Grundrechte. Weltanschauliche und gesellschaftspolitische Aspekte* (1974); *Konservative und christdemokratische Parteien in Europa. Geschichte, Programmatik, Strukturen* (1981). A selection of his contributions to books and journals includes, among others: 'Bedingungen und Grenzen des Dialogs' (1969); 'Katholische Soziallehre— Möglichkeiten und Grenzen' (1969); 'Die neuscholastische Naturrechtslehre zwischen Antimodernismus und moderner Sozialwissenschaft' (1974); 'Christliches Menschenbild—Theorem oder reale Möglichkeit gesellschaftlicher Lebensgestaltung' (1977); 'Katholische Soziallehre und Sozialismus' (1977); 'Christliche Demokratie und Konservatismus' (1981); 'Christliche Grundhaltungen in der Grundwerte- und Pluralismusdebatte der Gegenwart' (1983); 'Christlich-demokratische Programmatik und der Typus Volkspartei' (1984).

KARL-EGON LÖNNE, who was born in Wevelinghoven in 1933, studied history, German and Latin at Marburg, Cologne, Munich and Naples. He gained his doctorate in 1964 under Franz Schnabel at Munich with a thesis on the subject 'Benedetto Croce as a critic of his times' (*Benedetto Croce als Kritiker seiner Zeit*, Tübingen, 1967). He worked as a research assistant at Saarbrücken and from 1970 onwards at Düsseldorf and gained his *Habilitation* with a thesis on Fascism as a challenge (*Faschismus als*

Herausforderung (Cologne/Vienna, 1981, Italian translation Naples, 1985). Since 1979 he has been professor of medieval and modern history at Düsseldorf. Among his other publications are: *Politischer Katholizismus im 19. und 20. Jahrhundert* (1986); and articles on German and Italian history in academic periodicals. He has lectured in Hamburg, Bonn, Luxembourg, Paris, Salzburg, Trent, and Turin, and has given series of lectures at the Istituto Italiano per gli studi storici in Naples. He is a member of the German and Italian associations of historians.

OTTO MADURO is a married lay Catholic. Born in Venezuela in 1945, he studied at the Central University of Venezuela and at Louvain, from which he obtained his MA in religious sociology and his PhD in philosophy *magna cum laude*. He has held academic posts in his own country and in the United States, where he is at present attached to the Maryknoll Institute. He has published four books on the general subject of religion and liberation, among them *Religion and Social Conflict* (1981), as well as more than sixty articles in reviews in America and Europe.

DANIELE MENOZZI was born in Reggio Emilia (Italy) in 1947 and graduated in Church history from the university of Bologna in 1970. He is a member of the Bologna Institute of Religious Sciences and has taught modern history and then Church history at Bologna University. He is editor-in-chief of the review *Cristianesimo nella storia*. He has studied the relations between Christianity and 'enlightenment' (*'Philosphes' e 'Chrétiens éclairés'* (1976)), between Christianity and the French Revolution (*Letture politiche di Gesu dall'ancien régime alla Rivoluzione* (1980)). He has also tackled in various essays the problem of the relationship between Church and society ('LEglise et l'Histoire' in *La Chrétienté en débat* (1984)) and the aftermath of the Council ('L'Opposition au concile' in *La Réception de Vatican II* (1985)).

RENÉ RÉMOND is professor of contemporary history and political science, teaching at the University of Paris X Nanterre and the Institut d'études politiques. Among his books are *Les Droites en France* and *Les Catholiques dans la France des années 30*.

ANDREA RICCARDI, born at Rome in 1950, is full professor of the History of Political Movements and Parties at the University of Bari (Italy). He has studied nineteenth and twentieth century Catholicism in Italy and Europe, with special reference to the opposition to Vatican I. In *Roma 'Citta Sacra'?* he dealt with the history of the Roman Church during Fascism and the aftermath of the second world war, and in *Il Partito Romano* (1983) he produced a study of the connections between Vatican circles and Italian politics. He has also written two research reports on the pontificate of Pius XII, *Pio XII* (1984), and *Le Chiese di Pio XII* (1986).

PABLO RICHARD was born in Chile in 1939 and is a Catholic priest. He holds doctorates in religious sociology from the Sorbonne and in theology from the Free Faculty of Protestant Theology in Paris. He is at present Titular Professor of Theology at the National University of Costa Rica and a member of the Ecumenical Research Department there. He takes an active part in the base communities of Central America. He has published eight books, including *La Iglesia Latino Americana entre Temor y Esperanza* (The Latin American Church between Fear and Freedom), and *Death of Christendoms and Birth of the Church* (1982).

CONCILIUM

CONCILIUM

CONCILIUM 1986

All back issues are still in print: available from bookshops (price £4.95) or direct from the publisher (£5.45/US$8.95/Can$10.95 including postage and packing).

**T & T CLARK LTD, 59 GEORGE STREET
EDINBURGH EH2 2LQ, SCOTLAND**